Dramascripts

Goat Song

A new play based on an ancient myth by
DAVID CALCUTT
with explanatory notes and activities

Nelson

Nelson
Nelson House
Mayfield Road
Walton-on-Thames
Surrey KT12 5PL
United Kingdom

The play was first commissioned in 1999 by Shropshire Youth Arts Network specifically for use in and performance by secondary schools.

Photographs copyright © Image Makers
Project management by Elizabeth Paren
Designed and formatted by Geoffrey Wadsley
Cover illustration by Dave Grimwood, Pelican Graphics
Printed by L. Rex Printing Co. Ltd, China

This edition first published by Nelson 2000
ISBN 0-17-432609-2
9 8 7 6 5 4 3 2 1
03   02   01   00

Acknowledgements
The authors and publisher are grateful for permission to include the following copyright material: extract from the *Bacchae and Other Plays* by Euripides, translated by Philip Vellacott (Penguin Classics 1954, Revised edition 1972) copyright © Philip Vellacott, 1954, 1972.
Every effort has been made to trace all the copyright holders, but where this has not been possible the publisher will be pleased to make any necessary arrangements at the first opportunity.

CONTENTS

Series Editor's Introduction   IV

Worldwide Dramascripts   V

Introduction   VI

GOAT SONG   1

Scene 1   1

Scene 2   6

Scene 3   15

Scene 4   30

Scene 5   37

Scene 6   40

Scene 7   61

Scene 8   67

Scene 9   84

Scene 10   90

Writing the Play   96

Looking Back at the Play   104

SERIES EDITOR'S INTRODUCTION

Dramascripts is an exciting series of plays especially chosen for students in the lower and middle years of secondary school. The titles range from the best in modern writing to adaptations of classic texts such as *A Christmas Carol* and *Silas Marner*.

Dramascripts can be read or acted purely for the enjoyment and stimulation that they provide; however, each play in the series also offers all the support that pupils need in working with the text in the classroom:

- **Introduction** – this offers important background information and explains something about the ways in which the play came to be written.
- **Script** – this is clearly set out in ways that make the play easy to handle in the classroom.
- **Notes** explain references that pupils might not understand, and language points that are not obvious.
- **Activities** – at the end of scenes, acts or sections – give pupils the opportunity to explore the play more fully. Types of activity include: discussion, writing, hot-seating, improvisation, acting, freeze-framing, story-boarding and artwork.
- **Looking Back at the Play** – this section has further activities for more extended work on the play as a whole, with emphasis on characters, plots, themes and language.

John O'Connor

WORLDWIDE DRAMASCRIPTS

Whether we look at the Caribbean or China, ancient India or medieval Europe, we find that cultures across the world and throughout history have had one fundamental thing in common: they have all created myths, legends and traditional tales, in an endeavour to make sense of their existence and to confront the most challenging issues of right and wrong.

Worldwide Dramascripts present some of the most exciting and intruiging examples of these tales in the form of lively and thought-provoking playscripts. These bring together figures such as Theseus and Rama, Anansi and Guinevere, Hanuman the monkey-god and the famous Lambton Worm.

With the exception of *Goat Song* – an original retelling of Greek myths in a single play – each anthology brings together three or four short plays with a connecting theme, raising questions about:

- right and wrong
- justice and retribution
- the nature of heroism
- the eternal tensions between brothers and sisters
- the joys and pain of love
- the never-ending need to escape.

Because they feature such basic human concerns the plays and activities in Worldwide Dramascripts offer opportunities for students to engage with issues of enduring significance while enjoying some of the greatest stories ever told.

John O'Connor

V

INTRODUCTION

BACKGROUND TO THE PLAY

Drama, as we know it today, had its beginnings several thousand years ago in ancient Greece. There, in small villages in the north of the country, once or maybe twice a year, festivities were held in honour of the god Dionysos. These festivities celebrated the god's birth, life, death and re-birth. The celebrations involved much eating, singing, and drinking of wine. They also involved rough-and-ready re-enactments of episodes from the god's life, mostly comic – and the more wine was drunk, the more comic they became. But the climax of the celebrations was the re-enactment of the god's death and his re-birth. As the goat was sacred to Dionysos – Dionysos sometimes took the form of a goat – one of these animals was ritually killed, and its flesh eaten. Then one of the villagers would put on its flayed skin, and take the part of the risen god. (It is likely that, in even earlier times, the man who wore the goat-skin and who took the part of the god, was himself killed.) The song that was sung in praise of the god's death and re-birth was called the Goat Song, and the term was later used to describe the entire celebration. What interests me is that this primitive drama seemed to encompass two extremes of human nature – our potential for joy and living life to the full, and our potential for extreme violence. It celebrated both life and death and saw them, not as opposites, but as equal parts of the same whole. One, it appears, cannot be celebrated or enjoyed without the other. It is from the ancient Greek word for 'goat song' that we get our word 'tragedy'.

What those early Greeks were confronting in their celebrations of Dionysos was their own potential for violence. They knew it existed, that it was deeply rooted within their natures. In confronting it in this way, they were attempting, I think, to put a kind of safety barrier around it, to contain it within the ritual. Because the problem with violence is that it always escalates. One act of violence always leads to another, so that soon it gets out of control and, like an avalanche crashing down a mountain, destroys everything in its path. We've only got to look at the many trouble-spots in the world today to see how this happens. And one of the reasons it goes out of control may be our refusal to admit that it's part of us. We want to think that it's somebody else who's the culprit, never ourselves. So we go on, blindly, striking out at those we believe have injured us, not seeing that we too are doing the injuring.

This is what happens to Erigone in the play. She starts out as an innocent victim, but ends up committing an act of vengeance at least as terrible as the violence committed against herself and her family. One of the questions I was attempting to explore in the play, was how to stop this cycle of violence in which we can so easily become trapped. And, like those early Greeks, I came to two conclusions: that any solution is only ever temporary, and that one of those temporary solutions may be art – in this case, the art of drama.

Drama is perhaps the most all-embracing of the arts – it contains within it storytelling, poetry, music, song, movement. And it has its roots, as I said earlier, in those primitive festivities in ancient Greece. So, in writing this play, I wanted to try and capture at least some of the essence of those early dramas, their rough-and-readiness, their juxtaposition of the comic and the tragic, the farcical and the poetic. I wanted to write a play that was deliberately ragged round the edges. To do this, I decided to adopt a number of different styles, drawn both from ancient Greek and early English theatre. (For more details about the styles see Writing the Play on page 96.) So, the play is a kind of celebration of theatre – in other words, a celebration of the creative and joyous aspect of our natures. But the story it tells is a tragedy of violence and revenge. It was the attempt to encompass those two opposites of human nature, to reconcile them within the dramatic form, that lies behind the writing of my own 'goat song'.

David Calcutt

HOW THE PLAY CAME TO BE WRITTEN

Goat Song is the latest in a series of new works for children and young people which Shropshire LEA has commissioned from professional artists. A fruitful partnership between the LEA and West Midland Arts, the regional arts board, has supported a scheme in which artists use a newly commissioned work as a starting point for workshops and residencies in schools. In all, about 20 new works have been commissioned since the scheme began in 1995.

The intention has been to establish a direct link between an artist's own work and their interaction with children and young people in schools. The experience of working with a professional artist for a day must be different in some way from the experience of working with an expert teacher. Not better, but different. If the artist, using their own work as a springboard, can engage the pupils in a creative struggle of their own, treating them as fellow artists, offering them an insight into the creative process, then the workshop will have real and lasting value.

This then is the background to *Goat Song*. Proposals were invited from playwrights for a new play for teenagers. The commission brief specified that the script should be challenging in both form and content. We wanted an antidote to the usual diet of 'teenage' drama, with its conventional assumptions about the things teenagers were interested in.

Three proposals were shortlisted, and the playwrights were invited to present their ideas to a panel of English and drama teachers. A few months after he was given the commission, David Calcutt met the teachers again to present an early draft of his script. When the script was almost finished he ran a couple of workshops for teachers and pupils, to give the script its first trial run. Finally, the script was handed over to the teachers for them to use in their own schools, either as a teaching resource or as a play for performance.

The success of this project, and in particular the involvement of teachers in the commissioning process, has encouraged us to repeat the experiment on a larger scale. Three education authorities – Shropshire, Stoke-on-Trent and Telford & Wrekin – are involved in our future plans, which also have the support of West Midland Arts. The result will, we hope, be more new works for young audiences and performers of the same high quality as *Goat Song*.

Neil Rathmell
Arts Adviser
Shropshire LEA

THE FIRST PRODUCTION

'Yet the only thing we should expect, is the unexpected.'
(Old Woman, Scene 10, *Goat Song*)

When we commissioned David Calcutt to write a play, he spoke of the themes he wanted to explore in it. I anticipated an interesting and unusual play, which would be accessible for young people. When the play arrived, however, I found that I had not 'expected the unexpected'. It was a revelation, a tale of huge proportions, a startling display of theatre's, and life's, extremes, yet funny too. Bringing it to life for a premiere tour with the membership of the Drama Centres was quite a challenging task! I had a cast of 20 who did not know each other, four vastly different venues, a technician, a designer and ten days to bring it all together.

The cast needed to be aware of the voice as a manipulative tool if they were to play each space well on tour, so I began each rehearsal with a physical warm up (a game of tag, a head to toe loosening exercise or a silly rushed improvisation) and a voice warm up. I focused them on controlling their breathing. We began with low, even and sustained 'ssss' sounds, graduated to simple Thai Chi, and then to saying a sonnet in one steady breath. This was followed by a resonance section when we focused on volume and projection. A chorus of hums turned into 'ah's, Initially the hum was focused on the lips, then the throat, moving into the chest and finally throughout the upper body. The next section focused on articulation through tongue twisters and lines of nonsense words: *tat tet tit tot tut; pap pep pip pop pup; bab beb bib bob bub.*

The final section returned us to the text. I tried to focus them on a different element of the play each day such as storytelling, choral speaking, speeches, or the fast humorous passages. Before the final performances this work proved to be invaluable as it became a ritual the performers relied on. It hailed our entrance to the play's world.

In the first two days of rehearsals we roughly sketched the play with entrances and exits, charging through without much care, trying to find a defining tone for each scene, without getting bogged down in specifics. My aim at this stage was not to block but to make the cast see the endless possibilities the play offered for each role, and to get them to try one or two of these before they settled on one.

The rest of that first week was spent slowly trawling through each scene refining and developing the piece as a whole. We would work on small sections in the morning and run it in the afternoon. We started hot seating a character at the end of the day. This allowed each person to look at their character in depth and let the others scrutinise their character's relationship to that role. We built on that analysis in the second week. Characters began to write letters to other characters, when not directly involved in rehearsal. Not only did this technique fill a gap in the day but it enthralled the cast and they continued with it right up to the last rehearsal.

The second week also saw us focusing on the pace of the many narratives. I had decided to do the Bull/God scene as shadow theatre. The bold silhouettes neatly got round the problem of having a bull turning into a god on stage. The effect was so good that we introduced many characters, such as Metaneira, Icarius and Katsaki in shadow as well. In the final piece the shadow scenes signified a movement to another story line which helped to make the play accessible to audience and cast.

It was the different narratives, with their individual tone and pace, that caused the most difficulties for the cast. The scenes with the low characters have a fast pace and are incredibly enjoyable to perform, since they jump off the page into performance. The sub or prequel scenes, such as Scene 3, Katsaki and young Dionysos, required a different level of performance, sitting beside the great hilarity. The dark side of *Goat Song* requires immense stage presence and force. At every performance the darkness of Demeter, who rips open Erigone's humanity, scared me. The year nine pupil who played the role discovered a stillness that was disturbingly powerful. Her performance was made stronger, darker by the strength of the comedy.

Too often plays written for young people underestimate them and are turgid for the teacher. David Calcutt has taken a theme which explores our innate humanity. Students cannot help but enjoy the humour of the low character scenes and be fascinated by the dark, sinister plot. Our cast developed a deep respect for the play and its writer. In their final evaluations each took the time to thank David or compliment the play, but the biggest compliment they paid was their familiarity with the text – they could prompt each other without a book!

At the end of the process I had a cast of friends, a tired designer and technician and four appreciative audiences. We had succeeded in our challenge and a lot more besides. I had watched the cast grow in themselves, seen their delight at the audience's rapt response and knew they had experienced theatre in an unforgettable form.

Bec Large
Youth Drama Development Worker
Shropshire LEA

Note: The activities can be found at the end of the play. They are incorporated into the author's notes on writing the play on page 96.

The photographs in this book were provided by Hannah Proctor and Leela Cotley of Image Makers. (Image Makers are a group of young photographers working with Sarah Davies, a professional photographer, at Belmont Youth Arts Centre, Shrewsbury.) The photographs were taken in July 1999 at Belmont Youth Arts Centre, Shrewsbury.

Director: Bec Large
Design: Jacqueline Leech
Lighting and sound: Jonathan Tritton

Cast:

ERIGONE	Gemma Ryan	**HOGSHEAD**	Richard Harrison
ICARIUS	Phill McKie	**WINDBREAK**	Joseph Seager
METANEIRA	Tasha Benbow	**THICKSTAFF**	David Shuker
DIONYSOS	David Shuker	**THE LAD**	Tom Davies
KATSAKI	Beth Moore	**HAG**	Rebecca Smith
YOUNG DIONYSOS	Athena Lill	**GOODWIFE**	Elizabeth Smith
AMPELOS	Hannah Lang		

THE CHARACTERS

(in order of appearance)

CHORUS *of villagers*.*

ERIGONE

ICARIUS *Erigone's father.*

METANEIRA *Erigone's mother.*

DIONYSOS

KATSAKI *a goat.*

YOUNG DIONYSOS

AMPELOS

BULL/GOD

WINDBREAK *a goat-herd.*

HOGSHEAD *a goat-herd.*

THICKSTAFF *a goat-herd.*

THE LAD *a goat-herd.*

HAG

GOODWIFE

1ST WOMAN

2ND WOMAN

3RD WOMAN

1ST DEVIL

2ND DEVIL

3RD DEVIL

OLD WOMAN/DEMETER

* *The Chorus can be of any size and number. For a large-scale production, the Chorus may be separate to the rest of the cast. For smaller-scale productions, Chorus members can also play the characters.*

PRONOUNCING THE NAMES

ERIGONE *Er-ig-own-ee*

ICARIUS *Ik-ah- ree-us*

METANEIRA *Met-an-ee-ra*

DIONYSOS *Die-on-ie-sos (This is the accepted Western pronunciation. The Greek pronunciation is Dee-on-iss-os.)*

DEMETER *De-mee-ter*

KATSAKI *Kat-sak-ee*

GOAT SONG

SCENE 1

A bare stage. In the centre of the stage, standing upright, is a cross made of two rough wooden poles lashed together.

ERIGONE enters. She carries the skin and skull of a goat. She drapes the skin over the cross-piece, and places the skull on top of the upright pole. She then moves round to stand in front of the cross.

ERIGONE	A child in the womb	1
	A knife at the throat	
	A flower in the tomb	
	The song of the goat.	

(She sits in front of the cross, and bows her head.)

(The CHORUS OF VILLAGERS enter. They bring onstage all the items of props and costume that will be used throughout the play. They lay them down, then speak to the audience.)

CHORUS Once upon a time the land died

This land, the land where we've lived forever   **10**

It died, and this is how it happened.

First there was the war, which lasted a long time and left many dead

Then a bad winter, when the sky froze and the earth was like iron

And when the spring came it brought no rain

Only a polished sky and a wicked heat

And a sun that seemed to have come too close

And the heat grew fiercer with the coming of summer

And a scorching wind blew through the dry grasses   20
The river shrivelled, the springs dried
The crops withered, the animals died
And then the land began to die.

Then we were afraid, for there was no one to help us
No foreign aid, no humanitarian airdrops
The world's press didn't come to cover our story
We were alone and we knew we were alone
And we wondered why this disaster had happened.
What had we done to deserve this terrible catastrophe?
What crime had been committed?   30
What crime had gone unpunished?
How had we transgressed?
How had we offended?
We asked, but no one answered
Nothing spoke, the sky was silent
We thought that we had been abandoned forever.

(ERIGONE speaks to the audience.)

ERIGONE   I know why this disaster's happened.

CHORUS   No one saw her arrive, no one knew where she came
from.   40

ERIGONE   I know the reason for this terrible catastrophe.

CHORUS   She was just there one morning, standing at the roadside.

ERIGONE   I know why you suffer. I know the cause of it.

CHORUS   As if she's just suddenly appeared from nowhere.

No foreign aid *I wanted there to be a sense that this story could be taking place here and now.*

transgressed *Violated or broken a law or code of behaviour. In other words, they believe what has happened to them is some kind of divine punishment.*

'No one saw her arrive, no one knew where she came from.'

(The CHORUS begin to gather around ERIGONE, looking at
her with curiosity.)

CHORUS   A young girl, she was, but with a hard look about her
          Her feet bare and bloody
          Her clothes stained and ragged
          Something foreign about her, too, a touch of the exotic   50
          And it was hard for us to understand at first what she was
              saying
          So we gathered in closer, and asked her to speak a little
              slower
          And she lifted her head
          And spoke again.

          (ERIGONE now turns and speaks to the assembled CHORUS.)

ERIGONE	I know why this disaster has happened. I know the reason for this terrible catastrophe. I know why it is you're suffering. And I know what it is that you can do about it. **60**

(The CHORUS now speak to each other.)

CHORUS	What's that she said? I didn't quite catch it. She said she knows why we're in this fix. She knows? How does she know? Maybe she's a prophet. Some kind of fortune-teller. She looks more like a beggar to me. Or maybe she's mad. There's a lot of them around.
ERIGONE	Listen to me. Let me tell you my story. When you've heard it you'll find it's your story as well.
CHORUS	What's she saying now? **70** She's says her story's our story. What's that supposed to mean? I don't know. Like I said, she's crazy. I think the sun must have boiled her brains.
ERIGONE	There are things that bind us. Secret webs weave our lives together. I'm the cause of your catastrophe, and you are the cause of my suffering and sorrow.
CHORUS	Her suffering? We don't want to hear about that! What's her suffering got to do with us? We've got enough troubles of our own. **80**
ERIGONE	Listen. I'll tell you. Listen to my story, then you'll understand. And then you'll know what must be done.
CHORUS	You never know, there might be something in it. And if there's a chance she can help us out. Let's give her a chance and hear what she's got to say.

(The CHORUS speak to the audience.)

So there on the bare earth
Under the blistering sky
And the sweltering sun

She tells us her story   90
And we listen
And what she tells us changes our lives forever.

(ERIGONE begins her story.)

ERIGONE   I was born a long way from here, many miles to the
north. There in the mountains I had home, where I lived
with my mother, Metaneira, and my father, Icarius. I also
had a pet goat called Katsaki. And though life was hard
there, it was simple and honest, and things went on
unchanging with the changing seasons. Until the day that
the stranger came.   100

SCENE 2

ERIGONE's father, ICARIUS, enters.

ICARIUS	What a lovely morning! The first of spring!	1
	It makes my heart and my senses sing!	
	Today I don't feel like doing a thing	
	But resting a while in the sun.	
	I'll just make sure that my wife's not about,	
	She wants me to work, and she'll give me a clout	
	If she finds that I'm not, and beyond any doubt,	
	I know I won't find that much fun.	
	It's a long life we have, and hard are its ways,	
	And a man can't be working for all of his days,	10
	There's times he must stop, and take comfort and ease,	
	And that's what I'm going to do.	
	She's nowhere about. The coast's all clear,	
	So I reckon I'll just sit myself down here –	
METANEIRA	*(Offstage.)* Icarius!	
ICARIUS	Damn!	
	(METANEIRA enters.)	
METANEIRA	Where are you?	
ICARIUS	*(To the audience.)* She's here!	
METANEIRA	There you are! I've been looking for you!	20
ICARIUS	I was just going to –	
METANEIRA	I know what you were doing!	
	You'll sit in the sun while the farm goes to ruin!	
	I'm telling you, husband, there'll be trouble brewing	

If you don't get up off your backside!

The door's off its hinges, and so is the gate!
The fence is all down, and the roof's in a state!

ICARIUS   Now, listen, beloved –

METANEIRA   No, you listen, mate!
Start working, or I'll skin your hide!   30

ICARIUS   Don't get angry –

METANEIRA   I'll get more than angry with you!
I'll get violent! Take that! And another one too!
And one more for luck!

ICARIUS   All right! That'll do!

METANEIRA   No, it won't! Take this for good measure!

When will your common-sense ever arrive?
When will you learn that to just stay alive
We must toil, sweat and labour, if we're to survive
On this mountain, and life's not for pleasure?   40

(She speaks to the audience.)

It may seem harsh to treat him so
And give him blows a-plenty,
But, if I didn't, then I know
Our stomachs would go empty.

For life is hard and it deals out
Much harsher blows than I.
So if I give his head a clout,
And make him yell and scream and shout,
It's done to make the lazy lout   50
Get up and get his finger out,
For work's what life is all about,
And that you can't deny.

(METANEIRA goes.)

7

ICARIUS	Oh, my head! Oh, my back!
	Oh, my poor ribs! They're cracked!
	I'm bruised and I'm battered!
	I'm torn and I'm tattered!
	Knocked black and blue,
	And I've lost some teeth too!
	How can I work
	When I can't even walk?
	My brute of a wife
	Has bereft me of life,
	So I'll have to lie down,
	Just here on the ground,
	With my face to the sky,
	And expire, and die!

60

(He falls down, flat on his back, and lies still.)

(DIONYSOS enters. He carries a roughly-cut wooden staff with vine leaves woven around it. He speaks to the audience.)

70

DIONYSOS	Here come I, a travelling-man,
	With dust on my feet and a staff in my hand.
	I've travelled far and I've travelled long,
	Looking for somewhere to start my song.
	With my tangled hair and my tattered coat,
	I'm here to sing the song of the goat
	A song of birth, and death, and love,
	Taught to me by heaven above
	And here on this mountain my song will rise
	To bless the rocks and rivers and skies,

80

---

expire *Another word for 'die'.*

8

And once my singing has begun,
The world won't be the same again.

(He sees ICARIUS.)

But what's this here down on the ground?
A pile of rags? A bag of bones?

Bird or beast or reptile or what?
Neither fish nor fowl, I'm sure it's not.

It looks like a man from the shape of his head,
And by his appearance, I'd say he was dead.   90

(METANEIRA enters.)

METANEIRA   Dead, did you say? Is this some kind of joke?

DIONYSOS   Can you see me laughing? It's certain he's croaked.

'It's true! I've killed him! I'm a murderous wife!'

METANEIRA	And just who are you, and where are you from?
DIONYSOS	A passing stranger, that's who I am.
METANEIRA	And you passed by and found him in this position?
DIONYSOS	I did, and he's dead, though I'm no physician.
METANEIRA	Oh, husband of mine! What did I do?
DIONYSOS	Are you saying his dying is down to you?
METANEIRA	I can't deny it! The guilt is mine!
DIONYSOS	It seems you've committed a terrible crime.
METANEIRA	It was no crime! There was no intent! To get him to work was all that I meant! But the blows that I dealt him have ended his life! It's true! I've killed him! I'm a murderous wife!
DIONYSOS	Don't weep and moan.
METANEIRA	Why not? I'm upset! I've laid low my husband!
DIONYSOS	There's no need to fret!
METANEIRA	My man lies murdered!
DIONYSOS	But I've got a cure That will bring back a man from the dead.
METANEIRA	Are you sure?

(DIONYSOS takes a bottle out of his coat pocket.)

DIONYSOS	This bottle contains Just a few vital grains Of a potion whose power Makes the mountains and flowers And there's more than enough Of this magical stuff To return him to you Fighting-fit, good as new.

100

110

120

METANEIRA	Then hurry, and give him this magical drink.
DIONYSOS	A few drops on his lips should suffice, I think.

(He pours some of the liquid into ICARIUS's mouth.)

There, it's done. Now we wait.

METANEIRA	How long?
DIONYSOS	Just a bit.

In a few seconds' time he'll be up on his feet.

(ICARIUS wakes, suddenly, and sits up.)   130

ICARIUS	Where am I?
METANEIRA	It's worked!
DIONYSOS	Isn't that what I said?
METANEIRA	My husband's returned! He's back from the dead!

(ICARIUS stands, and stares about him wildly.)

But look how he stares, how his eyes gape and gaze!
And he looks at the world like a man in a daze!

(She speaks to ICARIUS.)

Icarius! What is it? Are you feeling bad?

ICARIUS	Oh, what a dream! What a vision I've had! 140

From earth up to heaven I thought I did rise,
Beyond trees and mountains, beyond stars and skies!
And the gates of the firmament opened up wide,
And revealed to me all of the wonders inside.
The gods in their garden were walking their rounds,

 **firmament** *The sky above, or, as in this case, heaven.*

And the air all about them was filled with sweet sounds,
Music that plucked on the strings of the heart
And pierced the soul like a honey-tipped dart.
All manner of miracles there I was shown,
A silver snake coiled in the heart of a stone,   150
And a golden-bird perched on the branch of a tree,
That grew on the shore of a wide, shining sea,
And far in the distance, cities whose towers
Flashed in the light of bright dancing fires.
All that I saw was wondrous and fair,
But fairest of all was a wheel in the air
And the faster it turned the brighter it shone
Till all was ablaze and the vision was gone,
And I woke with a cry and found myself here,
With my heart set to break my face wet with tears.   160
Now I'm back in the world, and I've told you my dream,
But what I want to know is, what's it all mean?

METANEIRA   It means you've been dead and resurrected.

ICARIUS   Dead? That's not what I expected!
I don't understand . . .

METANEIRA   I'll tell you the rest
When we're inside the house.

ICARIUS   Who's this?

METANEIRA   He's our guest.
If it wasn't for him you'd be lying there still,   170
Not a breath in your body.

ICARIUS   What? Have I been ill?
My memory's gone, my mind isn't clear.
Will somebody tell me what's going on here?

METANEIRA   When you've had a sit down I'll explain it to you.
I'll leave nothing out, every word of it's true.

And then I think you'll understand
Why it is you owe this man

Your life, and take him by the hand
With all generosity.   180

Now go inside. Sir, you're our guest,
Our home is yours, take ease and rest
Before you leave, you'll have the best
Of our hospitality.

*(METANEIRA and ICARIUS go. DIONYSOS speaks to the
audience.)*

DIONYSOS   Now my singing has begun
Here, beneath this foreign sun,
And, though it's started, before it's done,
It will be heard by everyone.   190

*(DIONYSOS goes. ERIGONE comes to the centre and speaks to
all, the CHORUS and the audience.)*

ERIGONE   And so they brought him into the house,
This man, that I'd never seen before.
They gave him food and drink
And he sat at the table and ate and drank,
Quiet, reserved, seeming almost shy,
As my mother told the story of what had happened
And told it again, over and over.
But even the strangeness of the story was nothing   200
Compared to his strangeness,
Because there was something – unnerving about him,
Something not entirely human,
An animal quickness in his movements,
A beast-light that flashed in his eyes,
Something of the form and shape and danger
Of some creature that had come in out of the wild,

unnerving *Disturbing.*

And carried the wild still deep in its soul.
And I trembled, I don't know whether from joy or fear,
And after my parents had shown him to his bed,   210
And after they had gone to their bed,
When the house was silent with sleeping,
I went outside and stood in the dark.

It was black night,
A full moon, the sky filled with stars.
I heard an owl screech,
I saw the huge, humped shape of the mountain rising
    above me.
Everything was still. Nothing moved. Everything was
    waiting.   220

And I spoke to the world around me.
I asked the grass and the trees, Who is he?
I asked the stones, and the wind that moved among the
    stones,
I asked the moon reflected in a pool of still water,
Who is he, who is he?
But if they spoke, I didn't hear them.

SCENE 3

ERIGONE leaves. KATSAKI enters and speaks to the audience.

KATSAKI   I'm Katsaki, the goat, and I know who this man is, and   1
                     the story of where he comes from. How do I know? Let's
                     just say that animals have a way of knowing things that
                     people don't. They have eyes that can see the story under
                     the skin. So I, with him. And now I'll tell you his story,
                     and this is how it goes.

                     Once upon a time, on the high slopes of a mountain in a
                     country far away, there lived a boy. He had no mother. He
                     had no father. He just lived on the mountain all by
                     himself, and he had lived there as long as he could   10
                     remember.

                     (YOUNG DIONYSOS enters and narrates.)

YOUNG DIONYSOS   He ate what the mountain gave him to eat. He drank
                     from its streams and pools. He lay on its grass in the
                     warm sunlight. He slept at night in the shelter of its rocks.
                     The mountain was his whole world, and he was the only
                     living thing in it.

KATSAKI   And one day he was kneeling before a pool, gazing at his
                     own face in the water.

                     (YOUNG DIONYSOS kneels as if gazing into a pool.)   20

 **He had no mother** *See 'The Myth of Dionysos' on page 104 for the story of Dionysos's birth.*

YOUNG DIONYSOS	And he was thinking to himself how handsome he looked, how large and dark his eyes were, how smooth and soft his face was, how his long hair shone in the light.
	(AMPELOS enters and stands behind him.)
AMPELOS	When suddenly he saw another face. Another face beside his in the water.
KATSAKI	And he gasped, and he stared. He couldn't believe what he was seeing.
YOUNG DIONYSOS	He reached out his fingers towards this other face. He stretched out his hand to touch it –
KATSAKI	– and as the tips of his fingers touched the skin of the water –
AMPELOS	– it wrinkled and split and the face disappeared.
	(AMPELOS moves away from YOUNG DIONYSOS, who turns quickly, to see no one there.)
KATSAKI	And he was alone again on the mountainside.
	(YOUNG DIONYSOS speaks to himself.)
YOUNG DIONYSOS	This is some kind of evil spirit. Some goblin or devil. It came here to steal my soul! I'm going to fight it. If it comes here again tomorrow I'll catch this evil creature, and kill it!
KATSAKI	So the next day he hid behind a rock nearby the pool and he waited. He waited to see if the evil spirit would come. And it did.
	(AMPELOS comes forward.)
AMPELOS	It stood by the pool, and looked around, as if it was waiting for something. And then it sat down on the grass by the pool.
	(AMPELOS sits.)

30

40

50

YOUNG DIONYSOS   And the boy was just about to spring out from behind the rock, he was just about to grab the creature, and squeeze its throat, and kill it –

KATSAKI   – when the creature took out a flute and began to play.

(AMPELOS takes out a small, wooden flute, and plays a simple, haunting tune. YOUNG DIONYSOS stands slowly.)

YOUNG DIONYSOS   He'd never heard anything like it.

KATSAKI   A sound like no sound he'd ever known.

YOUNG DIONYSOS   The music filled his soul with sweetness.

KATSAKI   Drove away all thoughts of murder.   60

YOUNG DIONYSOS   And he knew this could be no goblin or devil.

KATSAKI   No evil spirit could make music like this.

'The music that boy makes when he plays his flute, it's beautiful, like nothing you ever heard.'

17

	(AMPELOS stops playing. YOUNG DIONYSOS approaches him.)
YOUNG DIONYSOS	Don't stop playing. Carry on. Play some more.
	(AMPELOS turns to YOUNG DIONYSOS.)
AMPELOS	Who are you?
YOUNG DIONYSOS	I could ask you the same.
AMPELOS	I asked first.
YOUNG DIONYSOS	But this is my mountain.
AMPELOS	Your mountain?
YOUNG DIONYSOS	Yes. And that's my pool.
AMPELOS	Your mountain and your pool?
YOUNG DIONYSOS	So the least you can do is tell me your name.
AMPELOS	All right. I'll tell you. My name's Ampelos.
YOUNG DIONYSOS	Ampelos. And where do you come from, Ampelos?
AMPELOS	I live in the village at the foot of the mountain.
YOUNG DIONYSOS	Village? What village? What is a village?
AMPELOS	You don't know what a village is?
YOUNG DIONYSOS	No.
AMPELOS	It's a place where people live.
YOUNG DIONYSOS	People? There are other people in the world?
AMPELOS	Of course there are. Didn't you know?
YOUNG DIONYSOS	I thought there was only me. I thought you were a goblin. I thought you'd come to steal my soul.
AMPELOS	I'm just a boy from the village. I look after my father's goats. Yesterday one got lost. I climbed up here to look for it, and I saw you, kneeling by the pool. I was frightened.

70

80

18

| | They say in my village that there are demons on the mountain. Wicked, ancient things. That's what I thought you were. Some demon from the beginning of the world. | 90 |

They say in my village that there are demons on the mountain. Wicked, ancient things. That's what I thought 90 you were. Some demon from the beginning of the world.

YOUNG DIONYSOS I'm not a demon!

AMPELOS Who are you then? What's your name?

YOUNG DIONYSOS I . . . I don't know. I haven't got a name. I just live here on the mountain.

AMPELOS Have you always lived here?

YOUNG DIONYSOS Yes.

AMPELOS Alone?

YOUNG DIONYSOS When I was very little there was a woman who looked after me. She was very old. One day she told me she was 100 going away. She said I didn't need her anymore. She said the mountain would look after me. Then she went, and it has.

AMPELOS Is that all you remember about her?

YOUNG DIONYSOS She used to sing to me sometimes, in a language I couldn't understand. It used to make me cry, it was so beautiful. But the music you played on your pipe was even more beautiful. Will you play for me again?

AMPELOS I can't. I have to go back home.

YOUNG DIONYSOS No! Stay here! 110

AMPELOS It's late. I must go back.

YOUNG DIONYSOS Then come and play for me tomorrow.

AMPELOS I don't know if I should. I shouldn't come back up here again.

YOUNG DIONYSOS Why not? You came here today, even though you said you were afraid of me. And you weren't looking for your goat this time, were you?

AMPELOS	No.
YOUNG DIONYSOS	So you'll come back again tomorrow, then.
AMPELOS	All right. I'll come back and play tomorrow. 120
YOUNG DIONYSOS	Take my hand. Promise.
	(AMPELOS grips YOUNG DIONYSOS's hand.)
AMPELOS	I promise.
YOUNG DIONYSOS	Now you must come back.
	(YOUNG DIONYSOS looses AMPELOS's hand. AMPELOS turns from him as KATSAKI narrates.)
KATSAKI	So Ampelos went back to his village. But he didn't tell anyone about meeting the wild boy on the mountain.
AMPELOS	Because part of him was still afraid.
KATSAKI	And even though that night he had evil dreams – 130
AMPELOS	Where the darkness swarmed with bat-faced creatures –
KATSAKI	With wings and scales and snakes for hair –.
AMPELOS	And these creatures were all around him, screeching for his blood –
KATSAKI	And even though he woke covered in sweat –
AMPELOS	And feeling that his soul had been ripped out by its roots –
KATSAKI	He shook the dreams off like an old skin, and, with the rising of the sun, he took out his goats and went back up the mountain, where he found the wild boy waiting for 140 him.
	(AMPELOS and YOUNG DIONYSOS turn to each other again.)
YOUNG DIONYSOS	And as he had promised, he played for him. Day after day he went back, and each day, he played.

(AMPELOS plays the flute. DIONYSOS sits and listens as KATSAKI narrates.)

KATSAKI   And this is what they said, the people from the village.
Those who lived out their lives in that sleepy little
nothing-much-ever-happens-here-and-we-hope-it-never-
does village in the valley, this is what they said when   150
Ampelos played.

(CHORUS speak as the villagers from the valley while AMPELOS continues to play.)

CHORUS   The music that boy makes when he plays his flute,
It's beautiful, like nothing you ever heard.
That lad can charm the birds off the trees,
The skin off the water,
He can charm the sun right out of the sky.

Sweet it is, and sad too,
Kind of gives you a longing deep inside   160
An empty ache, kind of, that opens up wide,
And then he fills it up again
And it makes you laugh, and it makes you cry,
And you don't know whether you're laughing or crying.
It makes you think of your mother the day she died.

I tell you, I've wild animals, tamed by his music
The most ferocious lion purring like a tabbycat,
Wolves doggy-licking his outstretched hand,
Sharp-tusked boars grunting like farmyard porkers,
The fiercest bear rolling at his feet and gurgling like a baby.   170

And that's not all.
One time I was up on the mountainside when I heard
    him playing
And like everyone else who hears it I had to follow it,
Those tumbling notes like a chain round my neck,
    dragging me on,

And when I came to the place where he was,

21

Well, I just couldn't believe what I saw –
Even though I'm telling you this now,
These words that I'm saying, I just can't believe them –   180
But they're true, on all that's holy they're true –
I saw him playing,
And there were trees and stones in a circle around him,
And they were dancing, the trees and stones were dancing.

KATSAKI   That's what they said, the people from the village down at the foot of the mountain, that's what they said when Ampelos played. But what the wild boy said was this –

(AMPELOS has stopped playing.)

YOUNG DIONYSOS   I wish I could play the flute like that. Is it easy?

AMPELOS   No, it's not easy.   190

YOUNG DIONYSOS   Not easy for you, but I bet it would be for me. I bet I could play it easily.

AMPELOS   No, you couldn't.

YOUNG DIONYSOS   I could! I can do anything!

(AMPELOS laughs.)

Why are you laughing? Are you laughing at me? Stop laughing!

(AMPELOS stops laughing.)

Give me your flute.

AMPELOS   No.   200

YOUNG DIONYSOS   Give me your flute, I said!

AMPELOS   Why should I?

YOUNG DIONYSOS   Because I told you to!

AMPELOS   That's no reason.

YOUNG DIONYSOS   Yes, it is! Now give it to me!

AMPELOS	I'd give you anything you wanted, anything you asked for. Except this one thing. I won't give you my flute.
YOUNG DIONYSOS	I'll take it, then.
	(He snatches the flute off AMPELOS.)
AMPELOS	Give me that back!
YOUNG DIONYSOS	No!
AMPELOS	Give it to me!
YOUNG DIONYSOS	Not until I've played it. And I'm going to play it better than you!
	(YOUNG DIONYSOS blows the flute. He makes a terrible noise.)
AMPELOS	Stop it! Stop! Stop playing!
	(YOUNG DIONYSOS stops.)
YOUNG DIONYSOS	There! You see? I played it better than you.
AMPELOS	No. It was just a noise. A terrible, awful noise! You can't play at all!
YOUNG DIONYSOS	That's what you think, is it?
AMPELOS	That's what anybody would think.
YOUNG DIONYSOS	I see. Well, then, if I can't play it, nobody will!
AMPELOS	What do you mean?
YOUNG DIONYSOS	I'm going to break it.
AMPELOS	No! You can't!
YOUNG DIONYSOS	Yes, I can! I can do anything I want!
AMPELOS	Please! Please don't break it!
YOUNG DIONYSOS	Why not? It's only a piece of wood. A silly piece of wood with holes in it.
AMPELOS	No. It's more than that. It's . . . everything to me. It's my heart and my soul.

210

220

230

YOUNG DIONYSOS	Your heart and your soul? This stick?
AMPELOS	Yes!
YOUNG DIONYSOS	All right. I won't break it. I'll give it back to you. If you bring me something in return.
AMPELOS	What?
YOUNG DIONYSOS	This flute's precious to you. So bring me something precious, and you can have it back.
AMPELOS	What kind of thing?
YOUNG DIONYSOS	I don't know! Anything, as long as it's precious. Whatever it is, find it and bring it to me. I'll wait here till the sun sets. If you're not back by then, don't come back at all.

(YOUNG DIONYSOS turns and moves away from AMPELOS, leaving AMPELOS alone. AMPELOS turns towards the CHORUS. They part as he moves between them, and then close around him.)

(KATSAKI steps forward.)

KATSAKI	And the wild boy turned away, and Ampelos set off across the mountain, to search for a gift for his friend. All day the wild boy waited for Ampelos to return, but he didn't. Evening came, and the sky grew red, shadows lengthened, night filled the mountain, and still his friend didn't come back.
YOUNG DIONYSOS	And he was going to break the flute, but he didn't. He just sat there in the dark. He sat there waiting for his friend to return. Until, at last, he grew tired, and his eyes closed, and he slept.
KATSAKI	And as he slept he dreamed. He dreamed that Ampelos came to him. He was covered in blood. His body was broken and mangled. He stood there before him, and spoke to him out of the ruined mess of his face.

240

250

260

(The CHORUS part to reveal AMPELOS, wearing a horrific, bloody mask. He approaches YOUNG DIONYSOS and stands before him.)

AMPELOS   I went looking for a gift for you. I searched everywhere, across the whole mountain. I couldn't find anything. But I didn't give up. I went on searching. At last I came to a place where a stream ran down out of a rock, and a thicket of trees grew close together. And there, standing in front   270 of the trees, on the other side of the stream, was a bull.

(An actor enters, wearing a bull-mask. AMPELOS turns to face the BULL.)

Pure white, it was. The most magnificent creature I'd ever seen. And it just stood there, looking at me. So I took a step forward, and another, and another, and still it didn't move. And soon, I'd crossed the stream and I was standing right in front of it.

(AMPELOS stands directly facing the BULL now.)

I reached out my hand and touched its muzzle. I could   280 feel its hot breath on my hands. I could feel the whole heat of its body like a great oven burning. And I knew I'd found the gift I was looking for. This bull would be my gift to you. So I stroked its neck, and the bull bowed its head, and I grasped its shoulders, and swung myself up, and I sat there, straddling the bull's back.

(AMPELOS turns to YOUNG DIONYSOS again.)

And that's when I knew, too late, my mistake.

(Suddenly, the CHORUS chant, at the same time beating rhythmically on drums.)   290

CHORUS   The bull rears up and buckles under him
And it's like the world's exploding around
Like riding the back of a terrible earthquake
And he's jerkthumped, tumbled into the air

Scrabbling with fingers, trying to climb
But he can't and he's falling into the ground
And the world with its hooves is smashing his body
Gored and stamped and thumped and pounded
His whole life's being ransacked out of him
And he lies on the ground, torn and broken   300
A bag of crushed and bloody bones
Scrapped on the wasteheap of the earth.

(The drumming stops and the CHORUS falls silent. AMPELOS speaks to YOUNG DIONYSOS.)

AMPELOS   And this is the gift I've brought. This is the gift I found on the mountain. My torn body, my broken bones, my spilled blood. Take it. It's yours. My gift to you.

(AMPELOS takes off his bloody mask and lays it at YOUNG DIONYSOS's feet. Then he turns and walks back to the CHORUS.)   310

(YOUNG DIONYSOS wakes and cries out.)

YOUNG DIONYSOS   Ampelos!

KATSAKI   He woke with a cry.

(YOUNG DIONYSOS picks up the mask.)

YOUNG DIONYSOS   Ampelos!

KATSAKI   He went searching for his friend.

(YOUNG DIONYSOS flings the mask away.)

YOUNG DIONYSOS   Ampelos!

KATSAKI   All over the mountain, but he couldn't find him.

YOUNG DIONYSOS   Ampelos! Ampelos!   320

KATSAKI   He came to the place of the trees and the stream.

YOUNG DIONYSOS   Ampelos!

KATSAKI   But there was nothing there, and he couldn't find him.

YOUNG DIONYSOS	Ampelos! Where are you? Ampelos!
	(The BULL speaks to YOUNG DIONYSOS.)
BULL	Why are you crying?
KATSAKI	He turned. He saw the bull standing before him.
BULL	Who are you crying for?
KATSAKI	The bull was speaking, the one from his dream.
BULL	What's all this shouting about?
KATSAKI	The white bull that had killed his friend.
BULL	Why all these tears? Why this twisted face?
KATSAKI	And he knew now that his dream had been true.
	(YOUNG DIONYSOS speaks angrily to the BULL.)
YOUNG DIONYSOS	Where is he? Where's my friend? Where's Ampelos?
BULL	You already know the answer to that.
YOUNG DIONYSOS	Where's his body? What's happened to it? What have you done with it?
BULL	It's returned to the earth it came from.
YOUNG DIONYSOS	He's dead. You killed him!
BULL	No. You killed him. You sent him here to me. His blood's on your hands.
YOUNG DIONYSOS	No! You killed him! And I'm going to kill you.
	(YOUNG DIONYSOS attacks him. But the BULL flings him back, without effort.)
BULL	You can't kill me.
YOUNG DIONYSOS	Yes, I can, and I will!
	(He attacks the BULL again, repeatedly, and each time the BULL flings him back without effort.)

330

340

27

BULL	You may as well try to kill the wind or the thunder. Kill 350 the sunlight and the rain. Kill the mountains and the rivers and the sea. Kill the dark of the night, kill the stars in the sky. For I am all these things.
	(Exhausted, beaten, YOUNG DIONYSOS looks up at the BULL. He speaks, breathless and panting with effort.)
YOUNG DIONYSOS	Who are you? What are you?
	(The BULL takes off his mask to reveal himself as GOD.)
GOD	I am God. I am your father. And you are my son, and your name is Dionysos.
	(KATSAKI speaks. As he does so, GOD takes YOUNG 360 DIONYSOS by the hand and raises him to his feet.)
KATSAKI	And as he spoke, he knew the truth of the words, and that his name was Dionysos and he was God's son. And God took his son by the hand and raised him up, and he told him of his birth to a mortal woman, and how from birth he had been hidden on the mountain, for the jealousy of God's wife, who wished to destroy him. All these things and more God told his son, as they stood there together on the mountain's back. And, at last, God said to his son – 370
GOD	Now you have done what you were born to do, And now you shall know what your destiny is. In this place of death, new life shall arise. From this boy's body a plant shall grow That shall bear his name and the fruit of his death, Whose juice shall be sweet as the blood of the boy, And all that drink it shall taste his death,

I am God *Zeus, the king of the gods in ancient Greek mythology.*

And taste the life that comes after death.
And their mouths shall be filled with the song of his death
The song of sorrow, the song of joy,   380
The song of the lifeblood, the song of the heartbeat,
And this gift you shall take to all humankind.
And as he was trampled so they shall be trampled,
And as he was torn so they shall be torn,
To set the blood pounding and set the feet stamping
In joy everlasting, and set free the song.

(KATSAKI speaks to the audience.)

KATSAKI   And it all happened just as God had said. A plant grew
from the ground where the boy's body lay, and he called
it after the boy's name – Ampelos, the vine.   390

YOUNG DIONYSOS   And so Dionysos learned who he was, and learned too the
making of wine from the grape, and he left the mountain,
that had been his only home –

*(DIONYSOS steps forward and takes over YOUNG
DIONYSOS's speech.)*

DIONYSOS   – and he took that learning, God's gift to humankind, and
with it he went wandering wide into the world.

KATSAKI   And that's who the stranger is, and that's the reason he's
come here, because these people will be the first to receive
this gift. And the outcome of that, you'll have to learn   400
from others.

My time here's done
All I'll say, I've said
And before this day's run
Its course, I'll be dead.

*KATSAKI, GOD, and YOUNG DIONYSOS return to the
CHORUS, leaving DIONYSOS alone facing the audience.*

SCENE 4

DIONYSOS speaks to the audience.

DIONYSOS
    And now you all know who I am,   1
    Half-god, and only half a man,
    We'll resume the tale of this woman and man,
    Not forgetting, of course, their daughter.
    I've stayed with them for quite a time,
    And for their kindness, made return,
    By introducing them to wine,
    Much sweeter than any water.

    And between you and me
    Even sweeter is she   10
    Than the fruit of this tree
    She'll be mine, wait and see.

    The way in which it came about
    Made them stare and gasp and shout
    For with my staff I gave a clout
    And struck a great blow on the ground
    And up there sprang, before their eyes
    A full-grown vine, God's holy prize,
    All hung with grapes, to their surprise,
    So full, and fat and round.   20

    She laughed with delight,
    Such a wondrous sight,
    She'll be mine by tonight
    You'll see that I'm right.

    They take the grapes, they squash them flat,
    They pour the juice into a vat,
    Let it ferment, and that is that,

The God-gift of wine is now theirs.
And now new life floods through their veins,
Like horses broken free of reins,   30
They race and stamp and shake their manes,
Set free from all worries and cares.

And while they share their bliss,
I'll share mine with that miss,
I'll take just a kiss –
And a bit more, I-wisse.

(DIONYSOS goes.)

(METANEIRA and ICARIUS enter. ICARIUS is drinking from a skin-bag of wine. Both are happily drunk.)

ICARIUS   Oh! What rapture! What joy!   40
I feel young as a boy!
I could run! I could skip! I could dance!
I could swing from a tree!

METANEIRA   Give that wine-bag to me!
And I'll join you, if I get the chance.

(She takes the bag and drinks.)

Dear husband, I think
It's a marvellous drink,
And it fills me with passion and fire!

ICARIUS   Me too, dearest wife.   50
Why, in all of my life,
I've not felt such burning desire!

METANEIRA   My soul's filled with bliss!

I-wisse *A medieval term meaning 'indeed'. The 'I' is pronounced short, as in 'ink'. I needed a rhyme for 'kiss' and 'miss' and, by sheer luck, this fitted the bill.*

ICARIUS	Come and give us a kiss! Let's make passionate love here and now! Let us writhe, let us roll . . . !
METANEIRA	Good God, bless my soul! I'd like to, but I can't recall how!
	My head's in a muddle! Let's make do with a cuddle, At our age that's more than enough.

60

ICARIUS	You're right, Metaneira. Just come a step nearer And – give me some more of that stuff!

(He snatches the wine-bag off her and drinks.)

METANEIRA	You rotten deceiver! I'll never believe you Again when you say that you love me!
ICARIUS	How it makes my head roar!
METANEIRA	I'll make your head sore!

70

ICARIUS	I can see the sky spinning above me!
METANEIRA	Give it here!
ICARIUS	No!
METANEIRA	You what? You drunken old sot.
ICARIUS	I want a bit more –
METANEIRA	You've had plenty!

(She takes the bag.)

Now it's my turn – You swine!
You've drunk all the wine!

80

ICARIUS	No, I haven't –

METANEIRA	You have! Look, it's empty!
	(She holds the bag upside-down.)
	Now what are we to do?
ICARIUS	I don't know about you, But I'm starving, and I want my dinner.
METANEIRA	There's none left, you great clot! Our guest's had the lot!
ICARIUS	All our food?
METANEIRA	Yes.
ICARIUS	The thieving old sinner! I'm weak on my feet! What I want is some meat, Boiled or roasted, to stuff down my throat.
METANEIRA	Don't give up just yet, Our girl's got a pet –
ICARIUS	What, the cat?
METANEIRA	No, you fool! The goat! Let's go now and kill it Find its life-blood and spill it We're just answering our natures' call. A goat's only meat On the hoof –
ICARIUS	Let's go eat! Offer God the goat's life!
METANEIRA	Cut its throat with a knife!
ICARIUS	Scoff the lot!
METANEIRA	Meat –
ICARIUS	Skin –
METANEIRA	Blood –

90

100

110

ICARIUS	Bones, and all!

(*ICARIUS and METANEIRA grab the skull and skin from the cross, hold them up triumphantly, then throw them to the ground and go.*)

(*ERIGONE enters. She is disturbed, distressed, looks about wildly.*)

ERIGONE   Who's there . . . ? No one . . . ssh . . . quiet, now . . . there, it's all right, there, there . . . No . . . ! Stop . . . ! Look at you! The state you're in! What have you been up to . . . ? Can't say . . . can't tell . . . it's a secret. But your face, your face is so dirty! I'll wash, then, wash my face.   **120**

'Offer God the goat's life!' 'Cut its throat with a knife!'

Here, in this pool, scrub it clean. What's that? That face
looking up at me out of the water? Whose is it? Not my
face, no . . . And what's happened to it? Something
terrible, something awful – I won't look at it! I'll make a
mask . . . carve a mask from wood . . . and I'll wear it, I'll
wear this mask – there, it fits perfectly . . . now I can
speak . . . now I'll tell.

*(She stands facing outward, her face impassive, and speaks,
in calm, measured tones.)*   130

There is a place upon the mountainside
Where ancient oak-trees grow, a shady grove
Close-clustered round the banks of a deep pool.
Small flowers grow there too, purple and red,
Whose perfume fills the air with rich, sweet scent,
And sometimes she goes there to pick those blooms,
As she did today. And as she did,
Was overcome by such a weariness
That all her limbs fell heavy, and she lay down
To rest upon the bank among the flowers   140
And fell into uneasy sleep. Half-dreaming,
She saw the sunlight sprinkled through the leaves
Like flickering sparks, dark shadows drifting
Like smoke that rises from the autumn fires.
She heard no sound, no gentle step disturb
The silence. And yet, as if the shadows
Had congealed to solid form, or a tree
Had shed its bark, to reveal the supple
Form within, a figure stood above her,
Man-like, but more than man, about whose head   150
The flecks of sunlight danced and gathered,
Whose gaze held hers transfixed. Then, with a gasp,

transfixed *Stunned, amazed, rooted to the spot.*

Too late she recognised that face, too late
The dark intent upon that face. She rose,
Fell back beneath his weight, struggled in vain,
A helpless bird caught in a hunter's trap,
That beats its wings and cries in hopelessness.
And at last
What strength she had gave out, and she gave in,
Endured the torment till the deed was done,   160
And she was left alone. And then she wept,
Till weeping too was done, and all was still.
The flowers bloomed as before, the silent oaks
Spread their boughs across the shining pool,
But all was hateful now, the flowers, the trees,
The waters of the pool, the earth itself, all
Deadly enemies, betrayers of her trust . . .
She, who never harmed a living creature,
She, whose thoughts and deeds were ever gentle,
Mild, compliant to her nature and her sex –   170
To be treated so – to be used – so – and cast aside –

*(Her composure begins to break as she tenderly lifts the goat-
skull and skin.)*

A sorry sacrifice – see here – and here –
The wasted scraps of human appetite – !
Poor creature! Poor thing! Who'll weep for her?
Poor torn and tattered, bruised, broken, bloody thing!

*She replaces the goat-skull and the skin on the cross, and
remains standing there.*

SCENE 5

The CHORUS now speak to the audience, each other and ERIGONE.

CHORUS   That's what she tells us   1
          Those are the terrible words that leave her lips
          And fill our hearts with horror of her story
          And though we feel pity for her
          Still, we tell her, we don't know what it's got to do with us
          We can't see how what happened to you
          Has anything to do with what's happened to us
          How your plight and ours are connected
          Except, maybe, they're both the work of God
          And, that being the case, what can we do? 10
          What can you do?
          God doesn't work by human rules
          Maybe he doesn't work by any rules at all
          To him we're just toys, playthings
          Or maybe creatures in his laboratory
          And if he has a plan
          If there's a purpose to the suffering he causes,
          He's subject only to his own passions and desires
          Passions and desires which he indulges at will
          Above and beyond our judgement and justice. 20

ERIGONE   Is that what you believe?

CHORUS   It's a conclusion we've been forced to come to.
          The evidence leaves us no alternative
          God is unjust because he is God.

          (ERIGONE speaks with sudden vehemence and fury.)

ERIGONE   Then I accuse him! I accuse God! Here, on this earth,
          before you all, before the hills and the trees, before the
          sun and the wind and the sky, I accuse God of crimes

against humanity! I stand here unafraid, as his accuser
and judge, and I will have justice; and, if not justice,   **30**
vengeance! And when you've heard my story out, when
I've laid all the evidence before you, then you'll
understand how the crimes committed against me, have
brought disaster down on you. And you'll accuse him too,
and also howl for vengeance!

CHORUS   So we knew there was more to come
What had happened to her wasn't the worst that had
    happened
And she was summoning the strength to tell it
She was drawing up from some deep well within her the   **40**
    brimming bucketful of necessary courage
And at last it was there, and she drank from it
And she began to speak

ERIGONE   This stranger – who now I know to be God's son – had
gone. He'd left us with his gift, and we didn't see him
again. Life returned to an appearance of normality. And
the time came for my father to take his goats further up
the mountain, to fresh pasture. He took some skins of
wine with him, to keep him warm at night, he said. I
watched him go in the early morning. I saw him making   **50**
his way up the green slopes of the mountainside. I heard
him calling to his goats. Then he was gone, and I couldn't
hear him anymore. I turned and went back into the
house. And I never saw him in this world again.

CHORUS   Because he didn't come back
That's what she tells us, he just didn't come back.
One week passed, and then another, and still he didn't
    return
So she went to look for him
She went up the mountain looking for her father   **60**
But she didn't find him.

ERIGONE   There was the shelter he'd made for himself, a few stones
piled together, to keep off the rain and the wind. There

were the cold remains of a fire, some stale scraps of bread, the empty, flattened wine-skins. Signs that he'd been there, and there'd been others with him. But he wasn't there now. And though I searched and I called, my voice came ringing back empty from the peaks above me, and I couldn't find him.

(The CHORUS speak to ERIGONE.)   70

CHORUS   What had happened to him?
                Did you ever find out?
                You say you never saw him again. Is that why you're
                    here?
                Have you come searching here for your father?

ERIGONE   No. I'm not searching for him. It's useless to search for
                him, because I know I'll never find him.

CHORUS   How do you know?
                You can't be certain.
                There's always a chance –   80

ERIGONE   Listen to me. Listen, while I tell you what happened. I
                searched until it began to grow dark. Night was falling. It
                was too late to go back down the mountain again. So I
                went into my father's shelter. I gathered some sticks and
                moss together. I lit a small fire against the cold. I sat
                there, close to the fire, gazing into the flames. And in the
                flames of the fire, I saw a dream. And the dream that I
                saw there was the dream of what happened.

                She sits, gazing into the flames of the fire.

SCENE 6

Two goat-herds, HOGSHEAD and WINDBREAK, enter, shivering with cold and complaining.

HOGSHEAD	God's blood, Windbreak, this cold doth play the blade with my flesh.
WINDBREAK	Marry, it hath a keen edge to cut out the colour of a man's guts.
HOGSHEAD	If it doth persist, I shall be old before my time, for I'll lose my teeth o'chattering.
WINDBREAK	'Tis not the cold plagues me as much as the breeze that blows with it. For it has found entrance in one end o'my body and exit in t'other.
HOGSHEAD	Aye, brother Windbreak, but the foul path it doth trace through thy muddy entrails gives it a nose on leaving that it had not ere it entered.
WINDBREAK	Go to! 'Tis not so foul a stench as that which riseth from the hell-pit of thy belly. Each time thou speak'st I must turn my face for fear of contagion.
HOGSHEAD	Thou liest in thy teeth, Windbreak!
WINDBREAK	Thy teeth liest in the mire, Hogshead, so discoloured they be with the rotten fruit of thy breath.
HOGSHEAD	I'll knock thee down an thou speak'st further.

1

10

a keen edge *A sharp edge.*

mire *Swamp.*

WINDBREAK	An thou speak'st further, thou shalt surely knock me down. The force o' thy breath alone shalt do't.	20
HOGSHEAD	Nay, the force o' my fist shalt do't, thus!	
	(He hits WINDBREAK.)	
WINDBREAK	Thou eater of decaying flesh! Take this for thy pains!	
	(He hits HOGSHEAD.)	
HOGSHEAD	And thou take this for thy evil farts!	
	(He hits WINDBREAK. They fall to fighting. THICKSTAFF enters, carrying a bundle of sticks.)	

'Thou eater of decaying flesh! Take this for thy pains!'

THICKSTAFF	How, now! What's this? Part, I say! Cease! *(He stops them from fighting.)* What's the cause o' these blows? Nay, tell me not, for't will be naught. What'er the cause, make peace. The weather's to blame. 'Tis sharp enough with us, without us being sharp with each other. Make peace, I say!
HOGSHEAD	Brother Thickstaff, for thee, I will. Here's my hand, Windbreak.
WINDBREAK	And here's mine, Hogshead. I swear from this time on, when'er thou speak'st, thy words shall be sweet as honey to mine ear.
HOGSHEAD	I thank thee.
WINDBREAK	Though, as misfortune has it, not to my nose –
HOGSHEAD	Why – !
WINDBREAK	A jest, brother, a jest!
THICKSTAFF	No more o'jests or quarrels. Here. *(He throws down the bundle of sticks.)* There's wood for a fire. Do you see if with your sparky natures you can make a fire from 'em.
HOGSHEAD	Windbreak shall do't. Let him just pull down his breeches and lay his arse o'er, and his wind shall ignite a very inferno –
WINDBREAK	Why, thou – !
HOGSHEAD	A jest, brother, a jest, in answer to thine.
WINDBREAK	Aye, well, then, so be it. We're quits.
HOGSHEAD	But in truth, brother Thickstaff, I see not how we shall persuade flames forth in the face o' this chill wind.

30

40

50

inferno *A raging fire.*

THICKSTAFF	The entrance o' that shelter shall afford protection. Place thou the sticks there.
WINDBREAK	I'll do so. And with this flint strike heat enough for us all.
	(WINDBREAK moves apart, and sets about trying to light a fire.)
HOGSHEAD	This shelter was made by thy cousin, was it not, Thickstaff? 60
THICKSTAFF	Aye, so it was.
HOGSHEAD	'Tis said he has a daughter.
THICKSTAFF	'Tis said true enough. He does.
HOGSHEAD	And hast thou seen her?
THICKSTAFF	I have, Windbreak, for my pleasure . . . and my pain.
HOGSHEAD	Why for pleasure and for pain?
THICKSTAFF	For pleasure that I have seen her, and for pain that I have seen her and no more.
HOGSHEAD	Why, is she passing fair? 70
THICKSTAFF	I'd make a fair pass at her if I had the chance. And teach her then the meaning o' my name. But this is idle dreaming. My cousin keeps her fast. *(He calls.)* Windbreak, how goes thy work?
WINDBREAK	Warm enough!
THICKSTAFF	Is the fire lit?
WINDBREAK	Aye, but weakly. It needs more breath than mine to lend it strength.

shall afford protection *Shall give protection.*

THICKSTAFF	Go thou, Hogshead. A gasp from thy ample gut shall set it blazing. Go to! Do not thou make crooked eyes at me! I jest with thee! Thy breath and his combined shall bring forth the flesh o'the flame.

80

HOGSHEAD	And why should not thine combined with ours bring it forth the faster?

THICKSTAFF	I must keep watch for the Lad. I set him to scour the traps I set after pasturing our goats. I'll warrant thy belly craves company and weight.

HOGSHEAD	Thou speak'st truly. Its poor voice groans within me.

THICKSTAFF	Then go, while I watch for the Lad to bring us meat for it.

(HOGSHEAD joins WINDBREAK, and they blow together on the fire. THICKSTAFF speaks to the audience.)

90

This is the very shadow of existence. To be so rough cast as to live and labour thus? A pox on him that fashioned us. 'Tis said that we're tossed weeping to this stormy world, and weeping still we quit it. And today I well believe't, for never have I felt such heaviness 'tween land and sky. How the mountain glowers, how the very air doth wind and moan about its crags, as if the voices of the afterlife did howl our fate unto the darksome earth. Last night I dreamed I feasted on a goat, glutting myself, and yet the creature lived, and cried out with human tongue as I ate: 'Feast on my flesh! Feast well! For soon I shall feed on thine!' Fie on't. 'Twill not leave me, but like a rat gnaws at my innards, and gives a gloom to my nature it's not wont to have. There's something of this day has doom in it, and I'll be glad to see it come to close.

100

(HOGSHEAD and WINDBREAK call out.)

to be so rough cast *To be so roughly made.*

it's not wont to have *It's not used or accustomed to have.*

WINDBREAK	The fire's a-lit!
HOGSHEAD	And blazes e'en in the icy jaws o'the wind.
THICKSTAFF	And in good time, for here I see comes the Lad. 110
	(HOGSHEAD and WINDBREAK rise.)
HOGSHEAD	Doth he carry ought?
WINDBREAK	Aye, I perceive he doth.
HOGSHEAD	Then by God's will and thine, Thickstaff, we'll not go without.
	(The LAD enters.)
THICKSTAFF	How now, Lad. Hast thy search been fruitful?
HOGSHEAD	Shall we have meat to make our bellies sigh and sag?
LAD	Aye and nay.
WINDBREAK	What mean'st thou, 'aye and nay'? Either we shall or we 120 shall not.
LAD	In truth, I have and I have not.
HOGSHEAD	Was't thou teach'st this ragweed to riddle, Thickstaff?
THICKSTAFF	Nay, 'twas none of my doing. Plain blows are more to my liking. *(He hits the LAD.)* Speak'st without forks, Lad, or thou shall be forked e'er dark falls.
LAD	It's the plain truth I speak! Some of thy traps were sprung and some were not. From those that were, I have, and from those that were not, I have not.
WINDBREAK	Show us plainly what thou hast, then. 130
LAD	I'faith I shall. For 'twere beyond any power to show thee what I have not.
THICKSTAFF	I'll show thee what thou shalt have. *(He hits the LAD.)* There's for thy saucy tongue that it shall keep itself unsalted. Come. Let's see the pickings.

(The LAD takes a scrawny-looking dead rabbit out of his coat and holds it up.)

LAD   Here. Thou may'st pick what thou can'st from this. A coney.

HOGSHEAD   A coney?   140

LAD   Aye.

HOGSHEAD   A single coney ?

LAD   Aye.

HOGSHEAD   A single coney only?

LAD   Only and all, no matter how many times thou may'st repeat'st it.

(THICKSTAFF hits the LAD.)

THICKSTAFF   And is this the sum and total of thy endeavours?

LAD   I'm afraid to say aye for fear thou wilt'st strike me again. But I shall dare all, and take what pains may come. Aye.   150

(WINDBREAK hits the LAD.)

WINDBREAK   In truth, this will make little addition to our hunger.

HOGSHEAD   I feel myself subtracted just to gaze on't.

(HOGSHEAD takes the coney and goes into the shelter.)

THICKSTAFF   There's more meat to be had from a slice o' the air than from this scrap o' rags. *(To the LAD.)* Thou'rt an upstart crow, to bring us such poor pickings.

(He hits the LAD.)

 **coney** *Old word for a rabbit.*

LAD	Nay, Father, 'twas not my fault!
THICKSTAFF	Then whose fault was it? Mine, dost thou say, for setting such poor traps? Have that for thy boldness!

160

(He hits the LAD.)

LAD	I said nothing – !
THICKSTAFF	And this for thy silence!

(He hits the LAD.)

LAD	Father, I pray, strike me no more!
THICKSTAFF	I'll strike thee an I like, and thou shalt not have the say of it!

(He hits the LAD.)

WINDBREAK   Thickstaff, why dost this Lad name thee Father?   170

THICKSTAFF   'Tis a mark of respect to one whom he knows to be his better.

WINDBREAK   And, truly, is it no more than that?

THICKSTAFF   Truly, no more.

WINDBREAK   Yet I have heard it spoke . . . I have heard it rumoured among those that indulge in such loose-tongued practice – myself, mind you, not being one such as them –

THICKSTAFF   Thou hast more wind issue from thy mouth than thy arse. What hast thou heard rumoured? To the point.

WINDBREAK   I'm approaching it –   180

THICKSTAFF   Then approach it directly and not by detour. Tell me, what hast thou heard?

 **not by detour** *Not by the long way round.*

WINDBREAK	That this Lad is the true issue of thy loins.
THICKSTAFF	'Tis true.
WINDBREAK	Thou admittest it?
THICKSTAFF	I admit 'tis true that so 'tis spoke. But do not admit that I bred this 'tween any woman's legs. For admittance breeds payment.
WINDBREAK	I take thy point.
THICKSTAFF	Between us both, so did his mother.
WINDBREAK	Nay, Thickstaff, not between us both, for I had naught to do with the act.
THICKSTAFF	'Twas naught so to me, for I got nothing of it.
WINDBREAK	God's truth, 'twould have been a sorry getting. For this lad is as like to thee as a twig is to an oak. Or a sparrow to an eagle. Or a stickleback to a whale. Or a rabbit to a –
THICKSTAFF	A rabbit! Aye! I had forgot it! Where is't?
WINDBREAK	Hogshead hath it.
THICKSTAFF	Aye, but where be Hogshead?
WINDBREAK	He was here but a moment hence –
LAD	He's in the shelter, there, and the rabbit with him.
THICKSTAFF	Belike he's jumped our thoughts and cooked it as we jawed. *(Calls.)* Hogshead!
WINDBREAK	Hogshead! Art thou there?
HOGSHEAD	Aye!
WINDBREAK	And is the rabbit with thee?
HOGSHEAD	Truly, it is.
THICKSTAFF	And cooked?
HOGSHEAD	'Tis so.

190

200

WINDBREAK	Then bring it out that we may all eat.	210
	(HOGSHEAD comes out of the shelter.)	
HOGSHEAD	Here I am.	
THICKSTAFF	Aye, we see thee, Hogshead.	
HOGSHEAD	An so thou should, seeing thou art not blind.	
WINDBREAK	But the coney, Hogshead.	
HOGSHEAD	Why, 'tis here.	
THICKSTAFF	I'faith, I cannot see it.	
HOGSHEAD	I'faith, Thickstaff, thou'd'st have keen eyes if thou could.	
WINDBREAK	Where dost thou have it, Hogshead?	
HOGSHEAD	I have it stored where it is safe.	220
THICKSTAFF	And where may that be?	
HOGSHEAD	Why, in my larder, which I carry constantly with me.	
LAD	I perceive the meaning behind these riddles. 'Tis plain, the fat knave hath ate the rabbit.	
HOGSHEAD	Fat, dost thou call me, boy? Knave? Here's for thy 'fat' . . . *(He hits the LAD.)* . . . and here's for thy 'knave' thou knave. *(Hits the LAD.)* I'd give thee a third, but thou hast spoken partly in truth. For in truth, I am fat, and in truth, I have ate the coney.	
THICKSTAFF	What? Thou hast ate it all?	230
HOGSHEAD	Now, there thou hast a moot point, Brother Thickstaff, for 'all' implies substance, it figureth amplitude, and this coney had almost no substance and has not added a paper's width to this amplitude of mine.	

 **it figureth amplitude** *It shows fullness or breadth.*

WINDBREAK	Thou'st ate the rabbit and left us with nought?
HOGSHEAD	'Twas nought before I ate it, and therefore have I left thee with nought thou hads't before.
THICKSTAFF	Thou rotund rogue! Thou stumbling sack! Thou more than ample villain! Thou bag of guts on unsupportive legs!
WINDBREAK	I'll call thee fat, aye, and call thee villain too, and give thee fat pains for thy villainy!

240

THICKSTAFF	And villainous pains I'll give thee for thy fatness!
	(THICKSTAFF and WINDBREAK make as if to beat HOGSHEAD. HOGSHEAD backs off from them, crying out.)
HOGSHEAD	Help! Murder! Ho! Help there! They will kill me! Help!
	(ICARIUS enters, carrying several skins of wine. He speaks to the LAD.)
ICARIUS	What's to do, here? Is there murder committed?
LAD	I pray so. With good fortune these three will all murder each other.

250

ICARIUS	For what cause dost thou say that?
LAD	For the cause of my head, which I fear must break if they do live much longer.
ICARIUS	That's no cause to wish a man's death.
LAD	If thou wore my head on thy shoulders thou'd say it was.
ICARIUS	Better thy head should break than good men should lose their lives. And for that cause I'll help it onward. *(Hits the LAD, then approaches the three goat-herds.)* Peace, good fellows. Peace, I say! Come apart! What's the reason for thy wrangling?

260

THICKSTAFF	Empty bellies.
WINDBREAK	Which two have and one do not.
HOGSHEAD	Thou'rt in the wrong. Mine is as empty as thine.

THICKSTAFF	Thou liest. There's meat in it enough.
ICARIUS	But 'tis not meet that you should come to blows for this.
WINDBREAK	The blows I'll give this thief shall meet with him.
	(Goes to hit HOGSHEAD. ICARIUS stops him.)
ICARIUS	No more of that! Are we not all brethren? Do we not have humanity in common?
THICKSTAFF	We have hunger in common, and 'tis that separates us from him.

270

HOGSHEAD	I say again –
WINDBREAK	Say no more, unless it be thy prayers –
ICARIUS	Listen, brothers! Listen to me! This quarrel hath no cause. For I have here that will satisfy all needs, and bring such joy to heart and soul that there shall be dissolution of all dissent.
THICKSTAFF	What, hast thou brought food with thee, cousin?
ICARIUS	I have.
WINDBREAK	And be it of the meaty sort? There's none but that variety will satisfy our several hungers.

280

HOGSHEAD	Nay, but let it have bulk. For 'tis only that which hath substance will fill this substantial bulk o' mine.
ICARIUS	Aye, it hath body and bulk, brothers. And yet 'tis most delicate, sweet, and tender. For it will fill up both thy stomach and thy soul, feed flesh, and amplify the spirit.
THICKSTAFF	What manner o' food is this, cousin?
ICARIUS	Tis both food and drink, yet more than equal in its substance to 'em both. 'Tis a wonder! 'Tis a delight! 'Tis a delightful wonder! Tis a most wondrous and wonderful delight! 'Tis –

290

WINDBREAK	Our stomachs wait on thy panegyrics, brother. Let me taste for myself.
	(He takes a wine-sack.)
HOGSHEAD	And I'll take this.
	(He takes a second wine-sack.)
THICKSTAFF	And this third makes mine.
	(He takes a third wine-sack.)
	Now we'll test the truth of thy claims.
WINDBREAK	'Tis no solid thing thou hast here.
HOGSHEAD	Liquid it is, most truly.
THICKSTAFF	And 't has a pungency that delights the nose.
WINDBREAK	And a colour like to the blood.
ICARIUS	Why, thou hast spoke true. Blood it is. The blood of God's own veins.
HOGSHEAD	Will you drink, brother?
THICKSTAFF	Aye, I shall. And so shall we all. Let's to't.
	(They all drink.)
WINDBREAK	Lord, but it hath a warmth to it.
HOGSHEAD	It cascades to my stomach like the heat o' the sun.
THICKSTAFF	And spreads e'en to the very extremities o' flesh.
	(They continue to drink, growing more and more affected by the wine.)

300

310

panegyrics *Flattering praise.*

pungency *Strong smell.*

WINDBREAK	This is proof more than a coat against the cold.
HOGSHEAD	And unlike a coat, it hath no heaviness to it. Rather it makes the wearer lighter.
THICKSTAFF	Certainly it hath a speed to rush so through the veins. Cousin Icarius, thou'rt to be commended for thy concoction. Here's my hand.
WINDBREAK	And here's mine. 320
HOGSHEAD	Take mine also, brother, and take it heartily, for thy potent liquor hath given me the strength of a bear!
WINDBREAK	It hath lent strength and body to my voice. I would roar. *(He roars.)* Hark! *(He roars again.)* I am like a lion! *(He roars again.)* I am a very roaring lion!
THICKSTAFF	Where's the Lad? Lad, come'st thou to me.
LAD	Nay . . . I am afeared . . .
THICKSTAFF	Afeared? O' me? Nay, do not hide. Why art afeared o' me?
LAD	If those two be like to a bear and a lion, then may thou be'st like to a wolf and devour me – 330
THICKSTAFF	Allay thy fears, Lad. I am no wolf. But I will tell thee that which I am. In truth I tell thee . . . I say to thee . . . I do confess I am thy father! And now shall I embrace thee!
	(He hugs the LAD.)
WINDBREAK	Why, here's a scene to stop the throat.
HOGSHEAD	And break the ribs with bursting.
WINDBREAK	I'm moved to treat thee likewise. Come, Brother Hogshead, let me embrace thee.
HOGSHEAD	And I'll return thy embrace, Windbreak, an for thou'rt the truest friend man e'er had. 340
WINDBREAK	Thy grip is strong, for it doth squeeze water from mine eyes.

HOGSHEAD	See too how it spills upon my cheeks and o'erflows unto the earth.
WINDBREAK	And thy tears, rich with love, shall fructify the earth.
HOGSHEAD	And so love doth beget itself, and causeth the world to move.
THICKSTAFF	Thou speak'st true, Hogshead – for the world begins to move beneath my feet.
WINDBREAK	So it doth, and roundly.
HOGSHEAD	It shifts, it sways, it rolls beneath my feet!
THICKSTAFF	'Tis like to gape wide and swallow us in!
WINDBREAK	I fall! Hold me, Hogshead!
HOGSHEAD	I would if I could find thee!
WINDBREAK	I'm here!
HOGSHEAD	Thou'rt there, but where am I?
THICKSTAFF	The fabric o' the world is rent! My dream proved true! The day o' reckoning's upon us!
ICARIUS	Nay, brothers! 'Tis not the world. These marvels are appearance only. For the liquid has the property of working on the brain, so to create fantasies and visions –
HOGSHEAD	We are bewitched!
THICKSTAFF	Spell-strapped!
WINDBREAK	Enchanted!
ICARIUS	Nay . . . nay . . .
THICKSTAFF	Aye! Aye! Thou hast stol'n our souls!

350

360

fructify   *Make the earth fruitful*

ICARIUS	Would'st call me a conjurer?
THICKSTAFF	Aye! And more! Thou'rt a sorcerer!
WINDBREAK	A wizard!
THICKSTAFF	A warlock!
WINDBREAK	A necromancer!
HOGSHEAD	A goat!
ICARIUS	I am no goat!
HOGSHEAD	Thou art! Thou art a goat! See, brothers! His legs grow hairy!
WINDBREAK	I see! And he doth grow hooves!
HOGSHEAD	And horns upon his head!
WINDBREAK	He is a goat! A most horned and hairy goat!
HOGSHEAD	Cut his throat and spit him! He'll make a goatish meal!
ICARIUS	This is thy fancy talking –
THICKSTAFF	He's no goat –
ICARIUS	Thanks, cousin –
THICKSTAFF	Can'st not see? He is the Devil himself!
ICARIUS	Nay – !
WINDBREAK	The Devil, aye!
HOGSHEAD	I know him by his hairy legs!
THICKSTAFF	He comes to take our souls!
WINDBREAK	King of lies!
HOGSHEAD	Lord of flies!
WINDBREAK	The fiend!
HOGSHEAD	The foul fiend!

370

380

390

THICKSTAFF	Beat him, brothers, as we are true men!
	(They begin to beat ICARIUS.)
ICARIUS	No . . . I'm no devil . . . I am a man . . .
WINDBREAK	Thump him!
HOGSHEAD	Knock him!
WINDBREAK	Break his teeth!
HOGSHEAD	Crack his skull!
THICKSTAFF	Kill him, and we shall be praised for ridding the world of evil!
ICARIUS	I am a man . . . nothing but a man . . .
	(They knock him down, and beat him savagely. The LAD crouches in horror, watching. ERIGONE rises, and speaks, as the beating continues.)
ERIGONE	I see them. I see what they do to my father. In my dream I'm standing there and I watch what happens. They beat him and they go on beating him. At first he cries out, but then he makes no sound. He's silent and he lies still and they go on beating him. I hear them grunting, I see the twisted looks on their faces, like something not human. And still they go on beating him, and I know this is no dream, this is real, this is what happened, and I'm watching it and there's nothing I can do about it.
	(They stop beating ICARIUS. He lies still.)
THICKSTAFF	Stop! Enough!
WINDBREAK	Indeed, it is more than enough.
HOGSHEAD	He doth not move. Nor do I think he'll move again.
THICKSTAFF	In truth, we have beaten the very life out of him.
WINDBREAK	I did not think the Devil should be so o'erpowered by mere humanity.

400

410

420

HOGSHEAD	Aye, but even in death see how he deceives, for his corse maintains th'appearance of our brother goat-herd, Icarius.
THICKSTAFF	E'en so, Hogshead, in truth I think 'tis him we have killed and no other.
WINDBREAK	What say you? He was no devil?
THICKSTAFF	No, but only a common man.
HOGSHEAD	He spoke truth, then. 'Twas that drink deceived our senses.
THICKSTAFF	Aye – and therefore, 'twas the drink that killed him.
WINDBREAK	Thou speak'st a-right, Thickstaff. The drink's to blame, not us. For had we not drunk it, we would ne'er have raised a hand to him.
HOGSHEAD	There can be no fault placed on us. For 'twas he gave us the drink . . . and therefore – if the fault for his death lie anywhere – it lies upon him.
THICKSTAFF	And grievously hath he paid for his most grievous fault. I'll think no more on't, for my conscience is clear.
WINDBREAK	So is mine.
HOGSHEAD	And mine too. But tell me, Thickstaff, shall we then leave the body here in view t'advertise his fault?
THICKSTAFF	Nay! For though we three know there is no blame to us – others, who have no knowledge of the potency of this drink, may not reason so.
WINDBREAK	That's wise, very wise. We'll bury him, then.

Line numbers: 430 (WINDBREAK), 440 (HOGSHEAD).

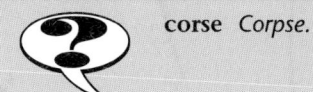

corse *Corpse.*

57

THICKSTAFF	Would that we could, but the ground is hard with frost and cold, and we have not the implements for breaking it. Therefore, 'tis my proposal that we divide the corse into fragments and scatter 'em freely about the mountain. Then, what the wolves do not eat, the crows may scavenge, and the jackals shall pick their teeth with's bones.
HOGSHEAD	Nay, I'll have naught to do with that – !
WINDBREAK	Wherefore sayest thou, Hogshead?
HOGSHEAD	I'm a goat-herd. My trade's not butchering. I ha' no stomach for't.
THICKSTAFF	Thou hast the stomach to stuff thy guts! Now shalt thou put it to bloodier employment! Thou'llt take thy share o' the task, man, for we are all one in this business.
WINDBREAK	And I think that, when we're done, we should quit this country entire, and go where our deed may not pursue us.
THICKSTAFF	Marry, we shall. Do you two now take the corse further off to a place more secluded, as 'tis fitting for such a bloody deed. I'll join thee presently, when I hath secured this place against discovery. Lad, go thou with them and give 'em assistance.
LAD	Nay.
THICKSTAFF	What dost thou say?
LAD	I'll have no part –
THICKSTAFF	Thine eyes have given thee part! What thou hast

455

460

wherefore *Literally, 'for why' or 'why'.*

witnessed makes thee party to the act, and so thou hast   470
duty to assist. And further, as I have confessed I am thy
father, thou'llt obey me!

*(The LAD joins WINDBREAK and HOGSHEAD, and they drag
off ICARIUS's body.)*

Now shall I scatter grass and sticks about, to make a
covering for his spilled blood. It grows dark. That's well.
'Tis the better cloak and season for these actions. Come,
thick night. Descend, and be the lightless mirror of our
darkening souls. Who's there? Is't someone? Who's
shadow is that? 'Tis thine own, and the form and fancy of   480
thine own fear. But what have I to fear? Go to, thou faint-
hearted knave! There's nothing. 'Tis but the residue of the
drink that doth distemper my brain. Then belike that
which hath been the cause, shall also prove the remedy.
(He picks up one of the wine-sacks and drains it.) There, now
my fears do gorge upon themselves and are thus
swallowed. And thus do I vomit 'em up. *(He belches.)* Now
I am myself again, I'll go and help the others with their
hacking work. *(He makes to go.)* Who speaks? I heard a
voice, then! The wind in the grass, no more. And yet   490
methought it had the very speech and accent of my
dream.

ERIGONE   Feast on my flesh. Feast well. For soon I shall feed on
                   thine.

THICKSTAFF   'Tis naught! Nothing! And even if it be aught – yet I'll not
                   hear or heed it!

(THICKSTAFF goes. ERIGONE speaks to the CHORUS.)

that doth distemper my brain *'Distemper' means to upset the health of
something. Thickstaff means that the drink is making him hear and see
things.*

ERIGONE

I woke from my dream. I was alone on the mountain.
It was morning. The fire was out. I lifted my arms to the
rising sun and swore vengeance on my father's killers.   500
I begged whatever god might hear me to grant me this.
Then I left the mountain. I did not return home. I forgot
my mother. Whatever god did hear me guided me and led
me on. I travelled the known world, I passed through
many countries still unknown. All was one to me, all
indifferent. I did not rest, I did not eat or drink. Desire for
vengeance was my nourishment. I went on, strong in the
faith that the god of vengeance would lead me one day to
the killers. And so I have been led to this place, to your
home. Because they are here. The killers are here. The   510
bloody-mouthed god within me tells me it is so. And this
is why your crops die. This is why war and plague have
come to you. You and your children, your homes, the
land itself are corrupted by their presence among you.
They are cursed, and their curse lies also on you, and that
curse will not be lifted until you bring me the killers who
live among you, and I have watched them die.

the bloody-mouthed god within me *Erigone personifies her desire for vengeance as a god living within her, hungry for the blood of those she pursues.*

SCENE 7

The CHORUS speak to the audience.

CHORUS   What she said stunned us   1
          We hadn't expected anything like this
          Her words were shocking
          We heard them but we couldn't believe them
          We heard them and but didn't want to believe them.

          (The CHORUS turn to ERIGONE.)

          Here, you say? Your father's killers here, among us?
          It's not true.
          You're wrong.
          It's simply not true.   10
          We'd know if there were strangers here.
          And there are no strangers here.
          We can't give any killers up to you because they're not
               here.
          There are no killers here.

ERIGONE   You're wrong. They are here. I know it, even if you don't.
          Your ignorance is no excuse. You suffer because they're
          among you. And if you don't give them up – or if you
          won't give them up – it doesn't matter. I'll find them. I'll
          walk among you. The god dwelling within me will sniff   20
          them out. He'll drag them by the hair into the light, he'll
          throw them down in the dirt at my feet. Let me through.
          Give me leave. I'll find them.

          (ERIGONE moves among the CHORUS, as they speak.)

CHORUS   She walks among us
          In turn she looks each one of us in the face
          And there's a light in her eyes that burns into our hearts

Like a candleflame searching every dark corner there.
And we can feel the power of that flame
We can feel the power coming off her   30
Wave after wave of shock voltage
Blasting us, searing the skin from our souls
Leaving us raw, naked and guilty
As if an angel of wrath were moving among us
With a command from God, to judge and condemn
With a blazing sword raised and ready to fall.

(ERIGONE suddenly takes hold of the LAD and drags him forward.)

ERIGONE   Here! Here's one! This boy! I knew the god would not fail
me! He's found this one! And where there's one, the   40
others will be found! Tell me, is this boy one of yours? Are
any here his parents? Has he lived here always? Or is he a
stranger, a new arrival?

CHORUS   The boy! We'd forgotten about the boy
He came here about a year ago
Just after the war started
One day he walked into the village, just like you
And in an even sorrier state than you
We thought he was a refugee, like so many others at that
    time   50
And we felt sorry for him, so we took him in
And he's lived here among us since then.

ERIGONE   There! You've said it yourselves! He came here when the
war started. The war, that was the beginning of all your
troubles. Don't you see? He brought the war with him! He
came dragging behind him all your disasters. He's god-
cursed, a killer, a carrier of plague. But he's not the only
one. There were others, as you know. Are they here? Have
you forgotten about them as well?

CHORUS   No. When the boy came, he came alone   60
There was no one else with him

	Like we said, he just arrived here, alone We're telling you the truth We've told you all we know.
ERIGONE	This boy will tell me the rest. *(To the LAD).* Look at me. I know who you are. I know you were with those that murdered my father. I see you don't deny it. Good. Now, what I want to know is, where are those men? *(The LAD just stares at her.)* Don't keep silent, don't try to protect them. We both know what kind of men they were. And I 70 know you had no hand in the crime. Tell me where they are, and all my vengeance will fall on them. *(Again, the LAD simply stares at her, uncomprehending.)* Did they abandon you? Did you run away from them? Are they hiding somewhere? Tell me! I'll make you speak! Answer me! Tell me what I want to know!
CHORUS	It's no good shouting at him No good saying anything to him He won't tell you anything He can't tell you anything 80 Isn't it obvious? The boy can't speak
ERIGONE	Can't speak? Or won't – ?
CHORUS	He's not spoken a word from the day he arrived And it's more than just not being able to speak The boy doesn't understand anything He's nothing more or less than an idiot.
ERIGONE	That's what he wants you to believe. To hide guilt and his shame he plays the fool. But he doesn't fool me! *(To the LAD.)* Do you hear? Do you understand? This mask you wear, I'll split it wide, and claw the truth with my nails 90 from your throat!
	(The OLD WOMAN steps forward.)
OLD WOMAN	Stop that! It's useless. He'll never speak to you. These people aren't lying. What you're saying makes no sense to

	him. Nothing to him has any meaning at all. His wits are gone through what he's suffered.
ERIGONE	What **he** has suffered – !
OLD WOMAN	You're not the only one in this world to have suffered. Many suffer, and there are many ways of suffering. Let him be. This tormenting of him will do you no good. He can't tell you what you want to know.
ERIGONE	Then who can? Who can tell me where my father's killers are?
OLD WOMAN	I can.
ERIGONE	You? Who are you? Do you live in this village?
OLD WOMAN	No. I'm a stranger, like you.
CHORUS	It's true. We've never seen her before We've no idea who she is, or where she's come from We're as much in the dark about her as you are.
OLD WOMAN	Who I am makes no difference. What you want is information, and I have it.
ERIGONE	Tell me, then. Where are they?
OLD WOMAN	Not in this world. They're dead.
ERIGONE	What? Dead, you say? You're telling me they're dead?
OLD WOMAN	Yes. A vengeance swifter than yours overtook them.
ERIGONE	I don't believe you!
OLD WOMAN	It's the simple truth.
ERIGONE	Nothing about you is simple, old woman. You're hiding something from me. In league with them, that's what you are, telling me this in order to protect them –
OLD WOMAN	What I'm telling you is no lie. They're dead.
ERIGONE	You tell me this – you appear, out of nowhere – why should I believe you? I know nothing about you –

100

110

120

OLD WOMAN	As a god guided you here, so a god guided me, and for the same purpose.
ERIGONE	What purpose?
OLD WOMAN	To reveal the truth.
ERIGONE	The truth! How do I know what that is? Your words don't convince me. If they are dead, then give me proof.
OLD WOMAN	I will. Here. Now. You'll hear how your father's killers 130 died. And you'll hear it from their own mouths.
ERIGONE	I don't understand. What do you mean?
OLD WOMAN	I'll call their spirits from beyond the grave.
ERIGONE	Raise the dead? You can do that?
OLD WOMAN	The god in me has granted me that power.
ERIGONE	Do it, then. Here. Now. Call them, if you can. And if you can, I'll hear them speak.
	(ERIGONE moves to one side. The OLD WOMAN stands central).
CHORUS	The old woman stood alone 140 She spoke softly to herself No one heard what she said, but we saw her lips moving And as she spoke, something happened Everything suddenly collapsed inwards As if a hole had appeared, and the world had fallen into it We felt the shock and jolt of it Everything fell apart and nothing made sense And then, in the same instant, it was over The hole vomited everything back up again And all was just as it had been before 150 But at the same time all was utterly different Because hell too had vomited something up

Smoke-shadows, grave-wraiths,
Earth's unholy inhabitants
Fleshless, bloodless, they stood there among us

OLD WOMAN   And I gave the command, and they heard me, and spoke.

grave-wraiths *Ghosts.*

SCENE 8

WINDBREAK, HOGSHEAD and THICKSTAFF have stepped forward from the
CHORUS. Each wears a death-mask. They speak in unison.

ALL	Death's dream kingdom where no voice cries	1
	The wasted land and the starless skies	
	And the fool weeps for those who thought they were wise	
	And stone tears drip from stony eyes.	

HOGSHEAD   Far we travel by journey afoot.

WINDBREAK   Heavy our going, sightless the wending.

THICKSTAFF   Ice-wind, iron-cold, bones froze to breaking.

HOGSHEAD   Stop we to rest at a place by the roadside.

WINDBREAK   Open to elements, affording small shelter.

THICKSTAFF   Bleak the landscape, bleak the souls waylaid within it.   10

(THICKSTAFF and HOGSHEAD become silent and still.)

WINDBREAK   Ach! I am sore a-flesh!
                     I think Death gnaws at my innards, makes him a nest in
                       my guts.
                     Even farts bring no fire but freeze fast to my arse.
                     I am too thinly-shaved, even to a paring.

Death's dream kingdom *This phrase is taken from T.S. Eliot's poem 'The*
Hollow Men':

> *'Eyes I dare not meet in dreams*
> *In death's dream kingdom'.*

wending *To move somewhere at a leisurely pace.*

a paring *A thin shaving.*

I walk about, stamp, flap my arms – then stop.

(He discovers the HAG lying curled on the floor.)

What's this, here at the road's edge?
Some huddle and jumble of rags.   2(
Some bundle and tumble of bags.
It lives! I stoop, peer closer. What kind of creature?
That breathes and snores and rasps so loud,
Crouched like a crabbed and crooked toad.
Withered and wrinkled and wart as a witch,
A wreck of a woman, a drab in a ditch.
How sleeps this crone so warm?
What keeps her safe from harm?
She's wearing a coat
That keeps the cold out.   3(
That coat'll soon be mine,
When I wake her with the toe of my boot.

(He kicks her.)

Hi! Wake! Arise!
Peel back your eyes!
The Day of Judgement's come!

(The HAG wakes, fearfully.)

HAG   Who's this comes a-disturbing of me this frost and
furrowed night? What are you? Some jack o'the dark?
Aroint thee, sprite, and spare an old dame's bones!   4(

aroint thee *A cry of protection given against an evil spirit or witch. It probably dates back to medieval times, but we know it only from Shakespeare's play 'Macbeth', in Act 1 Scene 3:*

1st Witch:
*A sailor's wife had chestnuts in her lap,
And mounch'd and mounch'd, and mounch'd. 'Give me,' quoth I:
Aroint thee, witch!' the rump-fed ronyon cries.*

What the term actually means isn't clear.

WINDBREAK	I'm none of them things, but master of 'em all. Old Nick's my name, and I'm Lord of Hell's Hall.
HAG	Have mercy, Lord Lucifer! What's want wi' me?
WINDBREAK	Naught but your soul, Dame Drab. And that I'll grab. The soul of a hag Will go well in my bag.
HAG	Aye, me! O, woe! Take not this soul from a wretched woman! 'Tis all I have! Lost and lorn and lone, I am, and naught but misery have I known! Yet have I never done **50** harm to any living creature! Wherefore should this crooked King of Hell come to catch me?
	Take pity, Lord Scratch. Go elsewhere for your pickings. This miserable mistress is not to your liking.
WINDBREAK	All right. Give us your coat instead.
HAG	My coat?
WINDBREAK	That's what I said! Give me your coat Or I'll throttle your throat.
HAG	I'll freeze without this coat on my back! **60**
WINDBREAK	Give it to me or I'll break your neck! It's freeze or burn in hell's black fire. You've got the choice. I think that's fair.
	(The HAG takes off her coat and gives it to WINDBREAK.)
HAG	You drive a hard bargain.

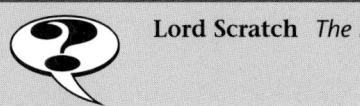 Lord Scratch   *The Devil.*

WINDBREAK	I'm not the devil for nothing.
	Now be gone!
	And take this boot up your bum for your pain!

(He kicks the HAG as she goes.)

	Was ever drab so direfully deceived?
	Was ever coat so wonderfully won?
	I'll put it on, and so defy this cold
	To do its worst.

70

(He puts the coat on.)

And thus it was that my life's blister burst.

(He freezes, remaining still throughout the following. HOGSHEAD and THICKSTAFF start to speak.)

HOGSHEAD	We wake to screams.
THICKSTAFF	Howls of anguish, harrowed with horror.
HOGSHEAD	And we see him burning.
THICKSTAFF	A coat of flames enfolding his body.
HOGSHEAD	He tears at the coat.
THICKSTAFF	But it clings to his skin.
HOGSHEAD	He claws at his flesh.
THICKSTAFF	It crackles and blisters.
HOGSHEAD	And the fire bites deeper, into the bone.
THICKSTAFF	And his lifeblood bubbles, smoking, hissing.
HOGSHEAD	And now he's not human anymore.
THICKSTAFF	Just a glowing mess of tumbling flame
HOGSHEAD	That runs about, and crumples, and falls –
THICKSTAFF	And lies still on the ground –
HOGSHEAD	Charred and blackened –

80

90

THICKSTAFF	As sparks and cinders drift on the wind.
HOGSHEAD	Then we take the still smouldering wreckage.
THICKSTAFF	Drag it to the roadside, dump it in a ditch.
HOGSHEAD	Cover it up with earth and leaves.
THICKSTAFF	And leave that place and go on with our journey.
WINDBREAK	And I begin mine.

To Death's dream kingdom where no voice cries
The wasted land and the starless skies   100
And the fool weeps for those who thought they were wise
And stone tears drip from stony eyes.

*(WINDBREAK steps back. THICKSTAFF and HOGSHEAD
continue their narrative.)*

HOGSHEAD	And one day we're walking through this barren country.
THICKSTAFF	And there's not a thing growing anywhere.
HOGSHEAD	Nothing, as far as the eye can see.
THICKSTAFF	Not a tree.
HOGSHEAD	Not a bush.
THICKSTAFF	Not a blade of grass. 110
HOGSHEAD	Nothing. Not a sausage.
THICKSTAFF	By which he means he's hungry. Which he always is. And he says to me, he says –
HOGSHEAD	I'm hungry, I says. And he says back to me, he says –
THICKSTAFF	What's new? I says. You're always hungry.
HOGSHEAD	Ah, yes, I says to him, but this time I'm really hungry, I says. I'm regular starving.
THICKSTAFF	And I says to him, you'll have to starve, I says, because there's nothing doing here.

HOGSHEAD	Starve? I says to him. Starve? I'm already starved! Look at me! Look at the thinness and raggedness of me! Look how the skin hangs and my body all bony! I'm not much more than a poor starveling skelington! 120
THICKSTAFF	Starveling skelington! I haven't never seen no starveling skelington with such a roundness of belly as I sees on you, I says to him. And there he stands with his belly all busting out of his belt in front of him, just like a great swole fruit about ready to pop.
HOGSHEAD	Once I had a belly, and so I did. But not no more. What belly I had has give up its ghost and gone long since with 130 the dear departed, and all that's left is this hollow shell of its former self. And I gives my belly a thump and it booms like a big bass drum, so it does.
THICKSTAFF	So there we are arguing it back and forth –
HOGSHEAD	And I says to him –
THICKSTAFF	And he says to me –
HOGSHEAD	And I says to him back again –
	(The GOODWIFE enters, carrying a large cooking pot and two ladles.)
GOODWIFE	When all of a sudden along comes a Goodwife, all rosy-cheeked and plumpy-armed and a-smelling of soap and 140 stew. And there she's carrying a great iron cooking-pot with her, and she plonks it down on the ground in front of the two of them, just like that.
HOGSHEAD	And that's the biggest cooking pot I've ever seen, I says, and I hope there's something in it.
GOODWIFE	To be sure there is, says she to him, and why don't you take a look in it and see for yourself?
THICKSTAFF	Just wait there a minute, says I to her. And who might you be, and where might you be coming from, in this 150 country where no one nor nothing lives?

GOODWIFE	And she to him says, I'm a Goodwife, and I have a little cottage just along the way there, which is for the rest and succour of poor starveling and way-weary travellers like yourselves.
THICKSTAFF	Further to that, I says, what brings you out of your little cottage along the road to us, a-carrying of that there pot?
GOODWIFE	I'll say to you sooth, says she to him. There's me in my little cottage, a-cooking up a nice pottage of stew, when I hears the two of you, a-moaning and a-groaning, and a-weeping and a-wailing and a-gnashering of your teeth in the very agony and want of hunger. And so, I thinks to myself, here am I a-cooking up this nice stew, and there's them poor souls in need of it, so I'll take it out to them before they perish for want of wittles. And no sooner said than done and here I am and here it is.
HOGSHEAD	A stew you say, I says to her.
GOODWIFE	Says she to him, a stew indeed.
HOGSHEAD	For us to eat, says I to her.
GOODWIFE	Says she, a feast for you to feed.
HOGSHEAD	And she hands me a spoon –
THICKSTAFF	And hands me one too –
HOGSHEAD	And without more ado, I take my spoon and I'm digging into that stew.
THICKSTAFF	But me, I say to the Goodwife, thank you gracious and most kindly, but I'll decline your generous offer, if it's all the same to you, only I don't have much appetite at

160

170

pottage *A thick stew made from vegetables, sometimes with meat added.*

wittles *Vittles, or food.*

present. Which isn't true, because I have, only there's something unease-making about this Goodwife and her pot.   180

HOGSHEAD   Not hungry? More for me, then. Give us your spoon and I'll eat enough for the two of us.

(He grabs THICKSTAFF's spoon and eats greedily.)

GOODWIFE   Belike you will, good master, quothes the Goodwife, and looks on all content and cheery as yon fine and famished fellow tucks in good and proper to his fare.

(HOGSHEAD continues to eat greedily.)

THICKSTAFF   And good and proper he tucks in too, shovelling the stew into his gob like his belly's dropped to the bottom of his boots.   190

HOGSHEAD   And no matter how much I eat . . . no matter how much of that stew . . . goes slobbering and slopping into my stomach . . . that there pot . . . don't seem to be getting any emptier . . .

GOODWIFE   And the Goodwife she ups and says, is somebody's eyes bigger than their belly? You eat all that up now like you promised, and don't you leave not but a single scrap.

THICKSTAFF   So he goes on with his gorging and stuffing of his face.

HOGSHEAD   And still that pot . . . don't get . . . any emptier.

THICKSTAFF   And I says to him, Hogshead, I says, you've had enough.   200

HOGSHEAD   And I says, no I haven't I says . . . while there's food to be ate . . . I'll eat it . . .

THICKSTAFF   But your belly must be full to busting now, I says.

HOGSHEAD   Full it might be, but so's this pot . . . and I'll be damned if I let any pot beat me . . .

THICKSTAFF   Damned you'll be, says I, for I smell witchcraft here.

GOODWIFE	Witchcraft! And what might you be meaning by that?
THICKSTAFF	Meaning that to my mind that there pot's bewitched.
GOODWIFE	Bewitched is it? And who might have bewitched it?
THICKSTAFF	None other than her that brought it!
GOODWIFE	Meaning me? she says.
THICKSTAFF	Meaning you, I says.
GOODWIFE	I never heard such, says she to he.
THICKSTAFF	Says he to her, you're hearing it now.
GOODWIFE	I'm slandered and scandalled, she says to him.
HOGSHEAD	Says I to them both, will you stop your row?

210

(He raises himself up from the pot, slowly, with difficulty.)

I'm finished and I'm full! What was in that pot is in my gut. Bewitched or not, there ain't no pot never beat me. And further to that, I says –

220

(He stops.)

And then I says no more, and they were the last living words I ever spoke in this living world.

(HOGSHEAD freezes, and remains still throughout the following.)

THICKSTAFF	For there in front of my eyes, his belly, swoll already to twice its size, proceeds to swell bigger and bigger.
GOODWIFE	And rounder and rounder.
THICKSTAFF	And fatter and fatter.
GOODWIFE	Till there's nothing of the poor man to be but belly. One great, round, fat and swoll up belly.
THICKSTAFF	And still that belly goes on swelling.
GOODWIFE	Still goes on, getting fatter and fatter.

230

THICKSTAFF	Till it seems it can't get any bigger.
GOODWIFE	Which it can't, without busting wide open.
THICKSTAFF	Which it does, with a great, ear-splitting, ground-thumping bang, a whumping explosion of guts that shakes the world and blots the sun, and I falls to the floor and I hides my face for pure human terror, for it seems like the end of all days has come. 240
GOODWIFE	Which for that one, poor soul, it has.
THICKSTAFF	And when at last it's all gone quiet again, I lifts my head and looks up, and I see . . . nothing.
GOODWIFE	Nothing. Not a sausage.
THICKSTAFF	Him as was once my mate has disappeared entire, blown and blasted clean out of this world, and not a mortal piece of him left to be found. So I picks myself up and dusts myself down, and says to myself, Thickstaff, I says, this is a strange and fatal country you've come to and you'd best be quit of it. And quit of it I am, taking the 250 road direct out of it, with only my wits for company, and which I'll keep shaved and sharp, for whatever further perils may await me on the road.
GOODWIFE	And with never a fond word of farewell to the Goodwife, he's gone down that road, which leads him at last to his end. As another takes to a different road, that wends and winds to a different place entire.

(The GOODWIFE picks up her pot and goes, as HOGSHEAD speaks.)

HOGSHEAD	Death's dream kingdom where no voice cries 260 The wasted land and the starless skies And the fool weeps for those who thought they were wise And stone tears drip from stony eyes.

(HOGSHEAD steps back. THICKSTAFF continues his narrative.)

THICKSTAFF   Now would I tell a tale of death most foul,
                       Slaughter and murther so unnatural
                       That all your nightmares were as childhood's dream
                       Compared to its most grim and gruesome horror.
                       Horror! Horror! It doth block my throat up   270
                       With a knot of blood, cleaves tongue to mouth,
                       Binds speech with heavy links of red-hot iron,
                       As I am bound below. I cannot heave
                       My soul into my throat, and have no words
                       With which to tell my tale. Therefore this lad,
                       Whom madness hath invaded and o'erthrown,
                       Bereaving him of sense and thought, shall speak.
                       By powers of darkness I command him,
                       By all the tongues of hell I give him voice.

                       (To the LAD.)   280

                       Dost hear me, boy? Thou miscreant knave, thou addled-
                       headed scarecrow! Thou straw-stuffed mannikin!
                       Rattlepan! Ragsbrains! Look upon me! Dost know me?
                       I am thy father's spirit! Speak'st thou for me. Relate the
                       details of this horrid tale, and my most horrid and
                       untimely death. A charm I'll wind to give thee power, my
                       hand upon thy head. Now let thy tongue's knot be
                       loosed, let memory untangle thy dazed brain, and wag
                       thy vocal-chords in comprehensive speech.

                       And to seal the charm and give it full of force   290
                       This blow shall set thee roaring on thy course.

                       *(He hits the LAD. The LAD cries out. He stares at the
                       CHORUS, and the audience, and then begins to speak.)*

---

murther *Murder. This speech is loosely based on the ghost's speech in
Shakespeare's 'Hamlet'.*

LAD

We're in a forest
Making our way through it
It's hard going
There's no path and we push through the undergrowth
Bramble, briars, thorns
It's hot and there's no light
And we're tired and thirsty   300
Face hands legs filthy with sweat and scratched by thorns
I wish we'd never come here
I don't know if we'll ever find a way out.

Then we come to a clearing
There it is suddenly ahead of us
Right there in what must be the centre of the forest
And for a minute the light's so bright suddenly I can't see
    anything
But I hear laughter
Girls' laughter   310
I think I must be dreaming
I rub my eyes, take my hands away from my face
And I see that I'm not dreaming
There in front of me there's a pool
And there are women in the pool
Three young women bathing
Bodies shining in the sunlight
As they stoop and cup their hands in the cool water
And splash it over themselves and each other
Laughing and singing and shaking their wet hair   320

I stand there staring
And I'm not the only one who's seen them
He's seen them too
He's standing and staring just like me
Then he gives a soft whistle under his breath
And that's enough.
The women stop what they're doing
They turn sharply and look at him
They stare right into him with their eyes

	And for a moment everything just stops dead	330
	It feels dangerous	
	Like there's going to be trouble.	
	But then they laugh again and lift their arms and hold them open	
	And they call to him and he goes walking towards them.	

(During the above the THREE WOMEN have entered. They speak to THICKSTAFF.)

1ST WOMAN	Sisters, see this mortal creature!	
2ND WOMAN	Perfect-formed in every feature!	
3RD WOMAN	An upright, proper form divine!	340
THICKSTAFF	That's me, ladies! I'm your man!	
1ST WOMAN	Shoulders so wide!	
2ND WOMAN	Legs long and lithe!	
3RD WOMAN	Thighs firm and strong!	
THICKSTAFF	And I'm really well-hung!	
1ST WOMAN	Come, man, see our opened arms.	
2ND WOMAN	Come, and taste our loving charms.	
3RD WOMAN	Be our darling, be our treasure.	
THICKSTAFF	I'm coming girls, and I'm packed with pleasure!	
1ST WOMAN	Feed our desires.	350
2ND WOMAN	Stoke our passionate fires.	
3RD WOMAN	Fill us up with delight.	
THICKSTAFF	I'll be at it all night!	
1ST WOMAN	Enter now into our bower.	
2ND WOMAN	Let us wrap you in our power.	
3RD WOMAN	Give yourself to love's sweet bliss.	

THICKSTAFF	I'm here! I'm yours! Now give us a kiss!

(The THREE WOMEN approach THICKSTAFF, alluringly, and place on his head the head and antlers of a stag, as they chant.)

WOMEN	With charms we enfold him

With charms we enfold him   360
With loveknots we hold him
We bind and we wrap him.
Ensnare and entrap him
Fix him fast with our gaze
Our prey and our prize
With tender caress
Loose the links of his flesh
In the flame of love's fire
Mould him to our desire

(THICKSTAFF is now wearing the stag's head.)   370

1ST WOMAN   The spell's done. Let him be!

(THICKSTAFF steps forward, proudly.)

THICKSTAFF   Look what's happened to me!

See my antlers proud!
Hear me bellow out loud!
See me stride, see me strut!
Watch me ravish and rut!
I'm all flesh and feast!
I'm all man, meat and beast!
I'm Lord of the Creatures, King of the Wood!   380

WOMEN   You're prey to the hounds, and we bay for your blood!

(The WOMEN are wearing dog-masks. Once more they approach THICKSTAFF, threateningly now and, as the LAD speaks, enact the killing of THICKSTAFF, either through stylised movement, or a series of still images.)

LAD   They're not women anymore
They're dogs
Women with dogs' faces

Fierce savage fangs bared and snarling
And he's a stag   390
A man with a stag's head and hooves where his hands
    should be
They bound after him
He turns and tries to run but he can't
He can't manage those hooves or the weight of those
    antlers
He stumbles under them they collapse about him
And he falls and they hurl themselves on him
Growling tearing at his throat ripping
At his flesh burying their muzzles in his body   400
I want to look away but I have to keep looking
And there's something mangled lying on the grass
There are bits and pieces of something scattered about
The bloody mouths of the dogs have tattered ribbons
    hanging from them
And still they're burrowing down deeper and deeper
Like they're looking for something down there
And they just go on biting a way through
Until at last they find it

(The THREE WOMEN have now removed the stag's head.   410
They hold it up.)

1ST WOMAN   His life, his soul's source.

2ND WOMAN   We found it and freed it.

3RD WOMAN   And sent it swift-footed to its only home.

(The THREE WOMEN have moved away from THICKSTAFF.
He speaks to the audience.)

THICKSTAFF   Death's dream kingdom where no voice cries
The wasted land and the starless skies
And the fool weeps for those who thought they were wise
And stone tears drip from stony eyes.   420

(THREE DEVILS burst on, wearing horrible masks.)

1ST DEVIL	Hast finished with our fare?
2ND DEVIL	Hast done with our damned delight?
3RD DEVIL	Thou'st had 'em time enough.
1ST DEVIL	And time now 'tis for their timeless torments.
2ND DEVIL	Our Master sends for them to be returned forthwith.
3RD DEVIL	Hell's empty and weeps hot tears for their absence.

(1ST DEVIL takes hold of WINDBREAK.)

1ST DEVIL   This one's mine! Come, Sir Foulfart. I'll give thee a hot wind shall make a volcano of thy arse!   **430**

(2ND DEVIL takes hold of HOGSHEAD.)

2ND DEVIL   And this is mine. Come, Sir Greedpig! I'll stuff thy gut to bursting with a meal of hot coals.

(3RD DEVIL takes hold of THICKSTAFF.)

3RD DEVIL   And I'm left with this. Come, thou Sir Lustloins! The pleasures of my pitchfork shall set thee to groaning.

1ST DEVIL	Take 'em, boys!
2ND DEVIL	Away with 'em!
3RD DEVIL	Shovel 'em back where they belong.

(The THREE DEVILS chant.)   **440**

DEVILS   In Death's dream kingdom where no voice cries
The wasted land and the starless skies
And the fool weeps for those who thought they were wise
And stone tears drip from stony eyes.

Our Master   *The Devil, again.*

(They laugh, horribly, and drag their victims away to hell. As they do so, the CHORUS bang drums and cymbals, blow on whistles, and so on, making a jarring, cacophonous noise, something like the noises of hell.)

CHORUS

Sinners go to hell
A crime's committed and heaven howls   450
Earth convulses with the horror
Sows the seed of righteous vengeance
And when it's ripe it's let to fall
A sudden weight dropped from the sky
Crushing those who have transgressed
And now we know that God is just
And all that happens has a meaning
Our lives are measured in the balance
And every act and deed is judged
And in the end all shall be well   460
And the innocent victim shall be avenged
And the suffering of the blameless shall be assuaged
And their rewards in heaven shall be assured
And the sinners, the sinners shall go to hell.

assuaged *Satisfied, appeased.*

SCENE 9

The OLD WOMAN speaks to ERIGONE.

OLD WOMAN	Now you know the truth. Now you know what happened 1 to your father's killers. You've seen with your own eyes, heard with your own ears. And all these people here, they're witness to it. Your father's death has been avenged. God tracked them down, brought them to justice. Vengeance has been taken. There's no reason for you to suffer anymore.
ERIGONE	No reason? No reason to suffer? I have every reason.
OLD WOMAN	What do you mean?
ERIGONE	My father's death is not avenged! And still the suffering 10 god in me cries out for vengeance!
OLD WOMAN	How? You've seen that justice has been done –
ERIGONE	There has been no justice to me! I was raped and my father was murdered! The injury that was done was done to me! And the wound of that injury still bleeds, and no hand but mine – not even a god's – can heal it!
OLD WOMAN	The three are dead. Payment has been made.
ERIGONE	Their deaths pay for nothing. The business is unfinished.
OLD WOMAN	What will finish it, then?
ERIGONE	Another death. 20
OLD WOMAN	Whose?
ERIGONE	The one who still lives.
OLD WOMAN	You mean this boy?

ERIGONE	Yes. I mean him.
OLD WOMAN	The boy's committed no crime.
ERIGONE	He was there with the others. He fled with them. He shares their guilt. While he lives the crime lives in him. While the crime lives the debt is still to be paid.
OLD WOMAN	You desire the death of an innocent child?
ERIGONE	Yes! Give me blood for blood! I'll have his life to pay for my pain!

30

OLD WOMAN	His life isn't just yours to take. It belongs to these people here. For the last year he's lived with them. They took him in to their care and protection. Unless they give him up to you, he's beyond your grasp.
ERIGONE	I'll speak to them. You'll see that they'll do what's right.

(ERIGONE speaks to the CHORUS.)

You've all heard my story. You know the injury that was done to me. You know what I have suffered. And you know how your suffering is one with mine. This boy is cursed. His coming here has infected your lives. The guilt for my father's death clings to him, a pestilence blighting this whole country. So there's a simple choice. His death or yours. A quick death for him, or the slow dying of yourselves and of your children. Which is to be? I've stated my case. It's up to you to decide.

40

(The CHORUS speak to each other.)

CHORUS	What can we do? What judgement can we give? The choice we've been given is no choice at all. I feel sorry for this boy – but he's not one of ours. He's a stranger, he came to us for help, and we took him in. That's right, he's a stranger – not of our blood or kin. And it seems he was involved in this killing.

50

85

If he didn't do the deed itself, he was there when it
   happened.
But it's a terrible thing to do, to give a child up to death.
We're all the family he has. Should we abandon him?
If we don't, we abandon ourselves, give everyone up for   60
   dead.
And if we die, this boy will die anyway.
Whatever we choose, his life's forfeit.
It seems we've decided, then. Do we all agree?
We haven't decided, it's been decided for us.
There's nothing we can do, we're ordinary people,
   powerless.
The responsibility is not ours.
Whether the boy lives or dies is between this girl and the
   god.   70
Let heaven seal his fate, we disclaim all obligation.
He's there.
What happens to him is out of our hands.

ERIGONE   You've reached the right decision. Judgement's been
made. All that remains is for the sentence to be carried
out.

OLD WOMAN   And you'll carry it out, yourself?

ERIGONE   Yes.

OLD WOMAN   Be the boy's executioner?

ERIGONE   Yes.   80

OLD WOMAN   You'll bear that burden of responsibility?

ERIGONE   Yes.

OLD WOMAN   Proceed then. No one will stop you.

(*ERIGONE walks towards the LAD. He is sitting, and has
reverted to his silent, mindless state. Between them ERIGONE
and the CHORUS describe the actions ERIGONE takes.*)

CHORUS   She walked towards the boy

She stood there a moment above him
He was playing with some stones in the dust
He took no notice of her   90
So with her hand she lifted his face towards hers.

ERIGONE   I look into his eyes, see nothing there, an emptiness
gazing back at me. Nothing to touch the soul with pity or
remorse. Two stones in a flat pool, hollow as my own
hollow heart.

CHORUS   Then she placed her fingers around his throat
Lightly, gently, almost tenderly

'As we watched, it wasn't him we felt sorry for. It was her.'

87

Like you do when you're placing a necklace around the
    throat of your daughter
But this necklace was deadly   100
And once fitted it would never come off.

ERIGONE   I begin to squeeze. I grip the back of his neck with my
fingers, press hard into his throat with my thumbs. I can
feel the strain on his windpipe. I can feel his whole body
suddenly stiffen with the shock of resistance. His eyes go
on staring into mine. I go on squeezing and pressing
harder.

CHORUS   He didn't appear to struggle
As if what little hold he had on life he was willing to give
    up   110
And strangely, as we watched, it wasn't him we felt sorry
    for
It was her. We felt sorry for her
We felt pity for her having to go through with this
Pity for the terrible thing inside her that was making her
    do it
There wasn't one victim being sacrificed, there were two
And her ordeal somehow seemed more awful.

ERIGONE   It takes a long time. Longer than I would have thought.
I have to use all my strength. I know the moment when it   **120**
happens. His body gives a jolt. I feel something break
inside him. And there's a heaviness, a weight I'm holding
onto, and I can't let it go.

CHORUS   She gave a final squeeze
His head arched back
A rattling sound came from his throat
Then nothing
His head hung limply
His whole body sagged
And she moved her hands from his throat   130
And held his dead body in her arms
She cradled it, like a mother cradles her baby

And she wept.

ERIGONE   What have I done? Why have I done this terrible thing?
This boy was guilty of no crime. He was innocent, and I
knew that. But I killed him. I've killed an innocent child.
Why? What drove me to it? I feel as if I've woken from a
bad dream – into a bad dream. I think of the day when
the stranger came to our farm on the mountain. Is that
when it began? Or was it long before? What event far   140
back in time set this chain of events in motion? And for
what reason? What purpose does it serve? How can I ever
know? Look, see here, look. All that you have suffered,
and all that I have suffered, see what it comes down to –
a girl crazed by pain and grief, and the broken body of
the child she's killed.

She holds the LAD's body and bows her head.

SCENE 10

The OLD WOMAN steps forward and speaks to the audience.

OLD WOMAN   If this tale was a tragedy, the story would end here. After   1
all, what is there after death? It would appear we've
reached the ultimate end of all human suffering, and that
there's nothing more to be shown or said. The drama's
done. Clear the stage of actors and bury the dead. This is
the ending we expect. Yet the only thing we should
expect, is the unexpected. And often, what we see as
journey's end, is in fact only a further horizon. So let the
dead remain unburied, for there **is** more to be said, as
these here now will testify.   10

(The CHORUS speak to the audience.)

CHORUS   It's true. There's more
But what happened next we can hardly credit
We thought we'd seen everything, but we hadn't
For now the Old Woman approached the girl
She approached her as she wept, and spoke.

(The OLD WOMAN speaks to ERIGONE.)

OLD WOMAN   Loose him. Leave him now.

ERIGONE   I won't . . . I can't . . .

OLD WOMAN   You've done what you came to do. Let him go.   20

ERIGONE   No . . .

OLD WOMAN   Leave him to me.

ERIGONE   To you?

OLD WOMAN   Yes. Your part in this is finished.

(What is described now by the CHORUS is enacted.)

CHORUS	She took the boy from the girl's arms
	She laid his body gently on the earth
	As if she were going to bury it herself
	Dig the hole with her own hands
	But she didn't
	She stood up and raised her arms across the body
	And she closed her eyes
	And she spoke.

30

OLD WOMAN She spoke in a language nobody knew. A language not of this world, that no human tongue knows. A language of the earth, of the dark under the earth, words dragged up from the roots of the earth, as if the earth had found voice and was speaking itself.

CHORUS And as she spoke the air sparked.

(There is a loud noise.)   40

Earth thundered.

(Noise again.)

Heaven roared

(Noise again.)

And a crack of white lightning split the sky wide.

(Final, climactic noise. The LAD wakes, rises and speaks.)

LAD And the boy rose. He stood. He looked around. He saw the sky. He saw the sun in the sky. He felt the rays of the sun warming his body, quickening his blood. He felt his heart beat, strong. He was awake and alive, as if death had   50 never taken him.

(The OLD WOMAN speaks to the LAD.)

OLD WOMAN	Death did take you, but I have brought you back from death. I am Demeter, goddess of earth, begetter of life, and I have given you this gift.
	(She turns to ERIGONE.)
	And to you too I've given this gift. Come here. Take this boy's hand. Take the hand of the boy you killed.
	(ERIGONE does so.)
ERIGONE	The girl did as the goddess commanded. She took the boy's hand. She clasped it in her own.	60
OLD WOMAN	Let the life with which I've quickened him quicken you also. It's a hard road you've travelled, a painful trail of suffering and tears. Now at last you have reached the end of that journey, and where you thought you'd find death, you've found life. And so it is for you all. For everything that lives has one purpose, and the life lived by one embraces all. And all that has happened has been for this. All that has been done, has been done for this.
	For death to make its transformation 70 In the place of sacrifice and redemption At this moment of mystery and revelation.
CHORUS	Then she was bathed in light She stood there before us, revealed, queen of heaven and earth And her light fell upon the boy and the girl Transformed and shining, perfect creations And not only them, the whole land was transformed The dead earth was no longer dead Leaves sprouted on the branches of the withered trees 80

Demeter *Demeter was the Greek goddess of growth, specifically of crops such as barley or corn. In some versions of the myth, Demeter was the mother of Dionysos.*

quicken *To animate, activate, fill with life.*

Springs of clear water bubbled up out of the rocks
Green shoots burst up through the parched soil
And what had long been a wilderness
Was a rich, rolling, fertile garden
A paradise blossoming and blooming about us.
But still the light grew, and grew stronger
And we saw those three figures
The old woman and the boy and the girl
We saw them as creatures no longer of flesh
But creatures of light, golden and holy.   90

LAD   And the air held them shimmering for a few moments
                  longer –

ERIGONE   Like reflections in water, flashing and rippling –

OLD WOMAN   Then the light faded, and they were gone –

                  (*They go.*)

CHORUS   And we were left here, witnesses to this mystery
                  Where the wind stirred the leaves and the birds sang
                  And earth blossomed its perpetual flowers.

                  (*The CHORUS sing to the tune of 'Lord of the Dance'.*)

                  We sing the song of the blessed boy   100
                  Who came to earth to bring us joy,
                  Heaven's darling, God's own son,
                  Man made goat, and goat made man.

                      Sing, sing, as loud as you can,
                      Sing of the goat who is a man,
                      Split his skull and cut his throat,
                      And sing with us the song of the goat.

                  He came to us as a little child,
                  He gave us wine and we all went wild,
                  'I bring the gift of life' he said,   110
                  So we knocked him down and killed him dead.

We ate his flesh and drank his blood,
We chewed his bones and we all felt good,
We scattered his ashes on the earth and then
He came back to life and jumped up again.

Sing, sing, as loud as you can,
Sing of the goat who is a man,
Split his skull and cut his throat,
And sing with us the song of the goat.

'I am the Lord of Goats!' he cried,   120
'I've lived and laughed and loved and died.
I was knocked down and then reborn,
Now I'm back and I've got horns.'

'All who live beneath the sky,
Are bound to walk until they die,
And the only way you can be free,
Is to sing the song of the goat with me.'

Sing, sing, as loud as you can,
Sing of the goat who is a man,
Split his skull and cut his throat,   130
And sing with us the song of the goat.

*(At the end of the song, the procession leaves, and the stage is
empty, except for DIONYSOS. He now steps forward and
speaks to the audience.)*

DIONYSOS   Our drama now has reached its end
And I come, in the guise of friend,
These final closing words to speak
Without deceit, disguise, or trick.
But plainly, as a fellow man
Whose mask is off, and tongue his own.   140
You've shared our sorrows, joy and pain,
Seen life lost and restored again,
Witnessed mysteries so great
They break the chains of human fate.
And though it may not all be true,

This play has been our gift to you,
And yours to us, to our relief,
Suspension of your disbelief.
Your rapt attention, and your pleasure,
These are the gifts that we most treasure.   150
But one gift more from you we crave,
One gift more, we pray you'll give,
A gift that heals all harms and hurts,
The warmth of your hands and the love of your hearts, –
For this keeps the world on its steady course,
And moves the sun, and the other stars.

DIONYSOS bows and goes.

WRITING THE PLAY

SCENE 1

This first scene, and the other 'chorus' scenes which appear throughout the play, are loosely based on ancient Greek theatre, where, at least in the earliest plays, the Chorus was the most important 'character'. The Chorus not only carried the story, they also commented upon it, gave their reactions to what happened, questioned the actions of the characters. They were a bridge between the actors and the audience, the voice of the audience onstage. As in those early plays, the Chorus in *Goat Song* is central and hugely important.

I wrote their lines in a kind of rough verse for several reasons. Firstly, the number in the Chorus is indeterminate; they can be few or many. Lines written in this way can be divided up and shared out to any number. Secondly, and perhaps more importantly, writing in verse places an emphasis on certain words and phrases that may not be there if they're written in prose, and gives the speech a rhythm that prose may lack.

WRITING: As a villager, write a short, detailed account of one of the disasters that befell your village, and led to its devastation. This won't be a detached piece of writing. You're recalling something that actually happened to you.

DISCUSSION: Discuss what you think the villagers' reactions are to Erigone when she first appears. How do they feel about her? Different villagers might have different feelings and reactions. You might try taking on the roles of the villagers, and discuss your feelings in this way.

SCENE 2

The style of writing in this scene – and in Scene 4 – is derived from that of the medieval mystery and mummers' plays. Mystery plays were short religious plays, written in verse, each one based on an episode or story from the Bible.

They were originally performed inside churches as part of the celebration of particular feast and saints' days, but later moved out into the town, where they were performed on large carts, or pageants, which could be pulled around the streets. Although they were religious, several of them contained a strong comic element. The mummers' plays developed even earlier than the mystery plays (a mummer is an actor). They possibly derived originally from pre-Christian, pagan beliefs. They were comic in nature, with much slapstick, and usually dealt with the death and return to life of one of the characters.

I've gone for the slapstick comedy in these two scenes, and have used a simple rhyme as part of it.

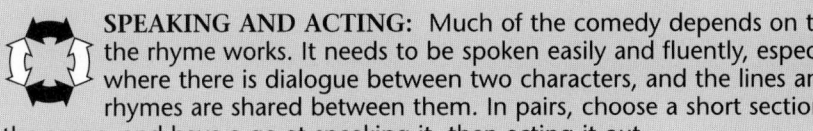

SPEAKING AND ACTING: Much of the comedy depends on the way the rhyme works. It needs to be spoken easily and fluently, especially where there is dialogue between two characters, and the lines and the rhymes are shared between them. In pairs, choose a short section from the scene, and have a go at speaking it, then acting it out.

READING AND DISCUSSION: Erigone's speech at the end of the scene completely changes the tone. Notice that, although she speaks in verse, it's unrhymed and irregular. Read the speech through, in groups or as a class, then discuss what you think Erigone's feelings are towards the stranger. Does she fear him? Is she attracted to him? Perhaps she feels a mixture of both.

SCENE 3

For this scene, which tells the story of Dionysos's childhood, I chose a deliberately simple, narrative style, in the manner of a folk-tale. Although Katsaki is the main storyteller, both Dionysos and Ampelos also tell the story. As well as speaking dialogue, they narrate their own actions, in the third person and the past tense.

You might find this idea of characters telling their own story a little unusual. It can also be a little difficult to play if you haven't done it before. The actor has to constantly switch between speaking as a narrator, and speaking as the character, almost as if he or she is playing two people.

READING AND ACTING: In threes, choose a short section from the scene, take on the roles of Katsaki, Dionysos and Ampelos, and read the section through a few times. Then try acting it out. After you've done this, discuss with the rest of your class or group how you think it worked, what difficulties you found, and how you might overcome them.

WRITING: Write a list of words and phrases that describe the character of Dionysos, and another list for the character of Ampelos. Compare the two lists. In what ways are the characters different, and in what ways are they similar? You could perhaps write a short piece comparing the two characters.

DISCUSSION: Ampelos senses that there is something dangerous about Dionysos. And, in many ways. Dionysos is unpleasant to Ampelos. But Ampelos still returns again and again to spend time with him. Discuss why you think he does this. Think in particular about Ampelos's life in his village, and what Dionysos might have to offer him that his life there does not.

SPEAKING: The Chorus describe in graphic terms the killing of Ampelos by the bull. How do you think these lines should be delivered, to create the greatest dramatic effect? Lines could be spoken by individual chorus members, or by small groups, or by the Chorus as a whole. Or you could use a combination of these. In groups, try speaking these lines in different ways, and see which you think is the most effective.

THINKING ABOUT STAGING: How do you think this scene might be staged? Music could be added, or simple percussion, or movement. Discuss your ideas, and then maybe write a piece about how you'd stage the killing of Ampelos in performance.

Scene 4

This scene once more begins in a comic, slapstick way, using verse and rhyme. But, from the start. there's something a little darker and crueller about it, and it builds towards the tragedy of the rape.

WORKING WITH THE TEXT: Have a close look at the opening of the scene, and see if you can find lines, phrases and incidents that hint at something darker and more serious to come.

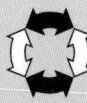

DISCUSSION: Look at the characters of Icarius and Metaneira. Are they different to the way they appeared in Scene 2? If so, how are they different, and what has made them different? What effect has the drinking of wine had on them?

DISCUSSION: When Erigone returns after being raped, her words at first are broken and disjointed, to indicate her utter distress. But, when she describes the rape, her speech is formal, almost objective. And she speaks of herself in the third person. Discuss why you think I chose to write the scene this way. How would it have been different if Erigone had described the rape in the first person, and in her distressed state?

ACTING: The acting of these two speeches by Erigone could be quite difficult, switching as she does from being very distressed to being calm and collected. One exercise you could try, working in pairs, is for one actor to play Erigone in her distressed state, and for the other to play the calm Erigone.

DISCUSSION: At the end of her long speech, Erigone's composure breaks down and she becomes distressed again, as she speaks these lines:

> A sorry sacrifice – see here – and here –
> The wasted scraps of human appetite!
> Poor creature! Poor thing! Who'll weep for her?
> Poor torn and tattered, bruised, broken, bloody thing!

Who do you think these lines are referring to? The killed goat, or herself? Or maybe both? Discuss your thoughts and ideas on this.

SCENE 5

We return to the Chorus of villagers in this scene, listening to Erigone's story. At first, they think they've heard the whole story. Then they realise there's more to come. At what point in the scene do they realise this?

WRITING: Having heard this first part of Erigone's story, do you think the villagers' attitude towards her has changed? As a villager, write a short piece describing your thoughts and feelings towards her, and how and why they've changed.

DISCUSSION: The Chorus try to justify, or at least understand, the injustice of Erigone's rape, with these lines:

> It's a conclusion we've been forced to come to
> The evidence leaves us no alternative
> God is unjust because he is God.

Discuss what you think they mean by these lines. What evidence is there in the world that might justify their belief that 'God is unjust'? Do you agree with them or not?

Scene 6

I wrote this scene in a kind of mock-Shakespearean language. The plays of Shakespeare, and other Elizabethan and Jacobean playwrights, grew out of the mystery and mummers plays. They also drew on the plays and poetry of classical Romans, which in turn were based on the works of the Greeks. So, in Shakespeare, we have a coming together of two traditions of theatre – medieval English and ancient Greek. It seemed right, therefore, to write this central scene in the play in the style and language of Shakespeare. There's something about the language, too, that lends itself to switching easily from low comedy to sudden tragedy. And it's very good for oaths, insults and swearing, without being too offensive!

WRITING: Bearing their names in mind, write a description of the three goat-herds, and give examples from what they say and do to support your descriptions.

DISCUSSION: Which of the characters in this scene (excluding Icarius), do you find the most sympathetic, and which the least sympathetic, and why?

COMPARING: Try taking a short section of dialogue, and re-writing it in modern English. As well as just 'translating' the words, try to get the sense of what is being said. Then read the dialogue, first in the original, and then in your modern 'translation'. Discuss how you think they compare.

THINKING ABOUT STAGING: How would you dress these three characters? Would it be in costume from the past, or modern dress? How would what they wear reflect or describe their characters? You could just discuss this, or, if you wish, sketch some costume designs.

READING AND WRITING: Read through Thickstaff's speech which begins: 'This is the very shadow of existence'. What do you think he's saying in this speech? What are his feelings about his life, and why does he have a sense of forthcoming doom? See if you can rewrite the speech, saying what you think he means in modern English.

DISCUSSION: When the goat-herds drink Icarius's wine, it has several different effects on them. Read through this section of the scene, then discuss the different effects it has, putting them in the order in which they occur.

WRITING: How do you think the goat-herds feel after they realise they've murdered Icarius? Different characters might have different feelings. Discuss this, or just think about it by yourself. Then write an account of the murder from the point of view of one of the characters, putting in that character's feelings about what's happened.

SCENE 7

WRITING: The villagers now know the whole of Erigone's story, and why she's come to their village. How do you think they react to her, now, when she walks among them, looking for her father's killers, and when she questions the Lad? Do her actions change their feelings towards her? As a villager, write down your feelings about Erigone as you see her now.

DISCUSSION: Several unexpected things happen in this scene, both for the villagers and Erigone. Discuss what these things are, and write them down. Which of them do you think is the most unexpected?

SCENE 8

In this scene, which shows the deaths of Windbreak, Hogshead and Thickstaff, I decided to use a mixture of writing styles, and to draw on different myths and folk-tales. Windbreak's death draws on the myth of the Greek hero, Heracles, and the manner of his death. Hogshead's death is drawn from a simple fairy-tale. And, for the death of Thickstaff, I drew on another Greek myth, the story of Actaeon, who was similarly changed into a stag and torn to pieces by hounds. The mixture of writing styles was intended to reflect this mixture of sources. The devils, at the end of the scene, come directly out of the medieval mystery plays.

 DISCUSSION: The manner in which each character dies is connected with their name and basic characteristics. Look again at how each character dies, and discuss how you think it suits them.

LOOKING AT STYLE: Look at the different writing styles used throughout the scene. Can you identify them? Discuss which ones you prefer, and why.

THINKING ABOUT STAGING: The way in which the deaths of the three might be staged in performance is indicated in the script. But there may be other ways. None of the deaths, however, could be staged in a realistic way. If you were directing this scene, how would you stage the deaths? Write a short piece explaining what you would do.

DISCUSSION: Do you think this scene is meant to be mainly comic, or does it have a serious side to it? Discuss which sections you think are comic, and which are more serious.

SPEAKING: The final Chorus speech, 'Sinners go to hell' is the climax of this scene. How do you think it should be spoken, to achieve the maximum dramatic effect? In small groups, try reading the speech aloud in a number of ways, until you've settled on the one you think works best. If other groups have done this, perform them for each other, and discuss how they compare.

SCENE 9

DISCUSSION: In this scene, Erigone demands the death of the Lad. Why do you think she does this, when she's discovered that her father's killers have already met their deaths? What is it, do you think, that drives her to want to kill this boy? What state of mind do you think she must be in? And does her killing of the Lad make her less sympathetic? As a class, or in groups, discuss the whole question of Erigone's behaviour in this scene, and whether you think it can be justified or not.

WRITING: Following on from this, as Erigone, write a short piece justifying your action. Or, as a villager, write a short piece condemning it.

DISCUSSION: The villagers are asked to judge whether or not Erigone should be allowed to take her revenge. Read through this section, and list the arguments they give for and against. Discuss how they reach their final decision, and whether you think it was the right one.

ACTING: The section where Erigone kills the Lad is written in an unusual way, with the villagers describing what happened in the past tense, and Erigone describing her own actions in the present. Why do you think I wrote it in this way? What dramatic effect do you think I was trying to achieve? In groups, try acting this section out, and then discuss how you think it works.

WRITING: Immediately after killing the Lad, Erigone is filled with regret. Why do you think this is? Read through her final speech, and then write a short piece in which you try explain Erigone's sudden change of heart.

SCENE 10

In this final scene, a miracle happens – the Old Woman, who is actually a goddess, brings the Lad back to life. This doesn't occur in the original story that was the basis for the play. In fact, the idea for this ending came to me quite late, as did the idea for finishing with a celebratory song.

DISCUSSION: Why do you think I decided to end the play in this way? How different would the play have been if there had been no miraculous resurrection, and no sense of celebration?

LOOKING BACK AT THE PLAY

1   **DISCUSSION: THE LANGUAGE OF THE PLAY**
Discuss why you think the play was written using different styles of language.
Does it make the play more difficult to read? Which do you find the easiest
style to read, and which the most difficult? How would the play have been
different if it had used only one style? Do you think having different language
styles adds to the play? If so, how? Which is your favourite style of language
used in the play?

2   **WRITING: CHARACTERS**
If you were an actor, being offered a choice of any of the roles in the play,
which one would you choose? Write an account of this character, describing
his or her characteristics, function in the play, and explaining why you would
find playing this character attractive.

3   **DISCUSSION: THE STORY**
Read through the story of Dionysos:

The Myth of Dionysos

Zeus, the king of the gods, took as his lover Semele, the daughter of King Cadmus of Thebes.
When Semele became pregnant with his child, Hera, Zeus's wife, and Queen of Heaven, grew
enraged, and was determined to take her revenge. She visited Semele, disguised as Semele's old
nurse. She noticed straight away that Semele was bearing a child, and asked her who the father
was. When Semele told her, she suggested that she prove to herself her lover was who he said
he was. And that she should do this by asking him to appear, not as a man, but as God, the
King of Heaven.

When Zeus next visited her, Semele begged him to grant her anything she wished. Not
realising what she intended to ask, Zeus agreed. When he heard her request he was horrified,
knowing that mortals cannot look on the gods in their true forms. He tried to dissuade her
from making this request, but she insisted and, having sworn an oath to grant her whatever
she wanted, Zeus was forced to grant her request. At the very moment he revealed himself in
his divine form, Semele was consumed by fire. But Zeus reached into the flame, snatched the
foetus that had been growing inside her, and placed it within his own thigh. There the child
grew, and was eventually born, as Dionysos.

Knowing that Hera would seek to destroy the child, he transformed it into a young goat,
and gave it into the keeping of the nymphs of Mount Nysa. There Dionysos was raised to
manhood, and there he discovered the vine, and the secret of making wine from its grapes.
There too he discovered his purpose – to bring joy and happiness to mankind through the
liberating effects of wine. The first mortal he introduced to this pleasure was the goat-herd
Icarius, and his daughter Erigone. During the drunken revels which followed, Dionysos raped
Erigone, and, later, when Icarius gave wine to some fellow goat-herds, they killed him,

thinking that he had bewitched them. Because of this, and because of the shame of her own rape, Erigone hanged herself.

Dionysos went out across the world, first to the East, then to the West, bringing his gift to all who would accept it. His followers – mostly young women – were known as Bacchantes or Maenads. They each carried a staff crowned with ivy, known as the thyrsos, wore the skin of a panther, and wound live snakes in their hair. Possessed by the power of Dionysos, they were driven into ecstatic frenzies, in which state they possessed unusual strength, and would tear apart the bodies of young animals. They also tore apart those men and women who refused to acknowledge the divinity of Dionysos. They also had the ability to perform miracles. When one struck the earth with her thyrsos, wine would sprang up. When one scratched the earth with her nails, a stream of milk flowed. And they could command honey to drip from the thyrsos itself.

When he came to Greece, Dionysos travelled from city to city, accompanied by his army of Maenads, demanding that all should accept him as a god, and practice his rites of worship. Those who refused were destroyed. Those who accepted him were granted visions and great joy. At Thebes, his mother's city, King Pentheus tried to outlaw his worship. Dionysos sent the women of Thebes into a crazed frenzy so that, thinking Pentheus was a lion, they tore him to pieces. Agave, Pentheus's own mother, entered the city bearing aloft her son's severed head in triumph.

Having converted all the cities on the mainland to his worship, Dionysos set off among the Aegean islands. He took ship from Icaria to Naxos but the sailors, not realising he was a god, set course for Asia, intending to sell him into slavery. Dionysos, however, turned the oars of the ship into snakes, caused a vine to burst from the deck and to enfold the mast, and entwined the sails in ivy. A panther and a leopard appeared on either side of him, and the terrified sailors leapt overboard into the sea, where they were changed into dolphins. Only one man, the helmsman, was spared, because he had spoken out against the kidnapping. This helmsman steered Dionysos to the island of Naxos, where he found Ariadne, daughter of King Minos of Crete. She had been abandoned by Theseus after having helped him slay the Minotaur. Dionysos married her, and, as a mark of favour, set her bridal crown in the heavens among the stars.

Dionysos's last act on earth was to travel to Tartarus, the underworld, where he persuaded Persephone, its queen, to release his mother's spirit. Dionysos then ascended to heaven with Semele, now named Thyone, to take his rightful place among the other gods.

All the cities in Greece continued to honour and worship Dionysos. It was in Athens, in the fifth century BC, that the first plays as we know them were performed during the yearly Festival of Dionysos.

Discuss the ways in which the elements in this myth – transformations, violent deaths, magical creatures, resurrection from the dead, frenzied and ecstatic behaviour – have been woven into the play.

4   **WRITING: AN OPENING SCENE**

Choose another episode from the life of Dionysos that you think would make a good play. Outline the episode, and say why you have chosen it. Then try working out a scenario (this is an outline of the scenes, and what happens in each one). You could then have a go at writing the opening scene. What title would you give your play?

5   WRITING: THE PLAY

Write a short piece about the section of the play which appeals to you most. Describe what happens in that section, and how it is written, then explain what it is about that section that you particularly like.

6   DESIGN: COSTUME

Although the story is based on an ancient Greek myth, the language and setting of the play encompasses many different time periods, including the present day. How would you costume the characters? Design a costume for one of the characters. Accompany your design with brief notes explaining it.

7   DESIGN: DESIGN A POSTER

Design a poster advertising the play. Think carefully about what image you will use, what meaning you want it to convey, and how it will attract people to come and see the play.

8   DISCUSSION AND WRITING: MUSIC

Music could well be an important element in a production of this play. Apart from the song at the end, where else might you use music, and what kind of music would it be? Discuss this, then choose two or three moments or incidents in the play that you think would benefit from having music added to them. Write a short piece describing these incidents, and explaining why you would use music there, and the kind of music you would use.

You could also perhaps try composing a few bars of one of these pieces of music.

7   WRITING: PROPS

If you were working on a production of the play for the theatre, what props would you need to collect? Some of the props are indicated in the script, but there may be others you would like to use. Make a list of all the props you would want, indicating which characters they are for, in which scenes they would be used, and how they might be obtained or made.

8   STORYBOARDING

Take one of the scenes in the play – it is best to choose a scene in which there is quite a bit of action – and storyboard it, giving a sketch of each incident, a caption stating briefly what is happening, and perhaps speech bubbles to indicate what dialogue is being spoken.

9   FREEZE-FRAME

Choose a scene from the play, and, in groups, storyboard it using a freeze-frame or still-life technique. A 'caption' could be spoken over each still-image, and characters in the still-image could speak key lines.

10   WRITING: A PRESS RELEASE

Imagine you work as the publicity officer for a theatre company producing this play. Write a press release, to go out to all the local papers. You need to briefly outline the play – without giving too much away – saying what it is about, what kind of play it is, and why people should come to see it.

11   READING

The Greek playwright Euripides wrote a play called The Bacchae in 407 BC. It was, in fact, his last play, and it deals with the story of Dionysos's return to Thebes and the killing of King Pentheus (see 'The Myth of Dionysos'). The translation by Philip Vellacott, in *The Bacchae and Other Plays* by Euripides, published by Penguin in 1954, is a good one to read. The opening speech by Dionysos gives a particularly good account of the god's birth and travels across Asia. Here is an extract:

'I am Dionysus, son of Zeus. My mother was Semele, Cadmus' daughter. From her womb the fire
Of a lightning-flash delivered me.
I have come here
To Thebes and her two rivers, Dirce and Ismenus,
Veiling my godhead in a mortal shape. I see
Here near the palace my mother's monument, that records
Her death by lightning. Here her house stood; and its ruins
Smoulder with the still-living flame of Zeus' fire –
The immortal cruelty Hera wreaked on my mother.
Cadmus does well to keep this ground inviolable,
A precinct consecrated in his daughter's name;
And I have decked it round with sprays of young vine-leaves.
From the field of Lydia and Phrygia, fertile in gold,
I travelled first to the sun-smitten Persian plains,

The walled cities of Bactria, the harsh Median country,
Wealthy Arabia, the whole tract of the Asian coast
Where mingled swarms of Greeks and Orientals live
In magnificent cities; and before reaching this,
The first city of Hellas I have visited,
I had already, in all those regions of the east,
Performed my dances and set forth my ritual
To make my godhead manifest to mortal men.'

For reading about Greek mythology in general, try:
Tales of the Greek Heroes by Roger Lancelyn Green (Puffin Paperbacks)
Myths and Legends by Anthony Horowitz (Kingfisher Books) [This also includes some non-Greek myths]
The Greek Myths: Complete Edition by Robert Graves (Penguin Paperbacks). This is an extremely comprehensive account of every Greek myth, from the earliest creation myths up to the story of the Trojan War and the wanderings of Odysseus, and one of the best of its kind.
There's also an excellent web-site on the internet called 'Greek Mythology Link'. The address is: http://hsa.brown.edu/~maicar/